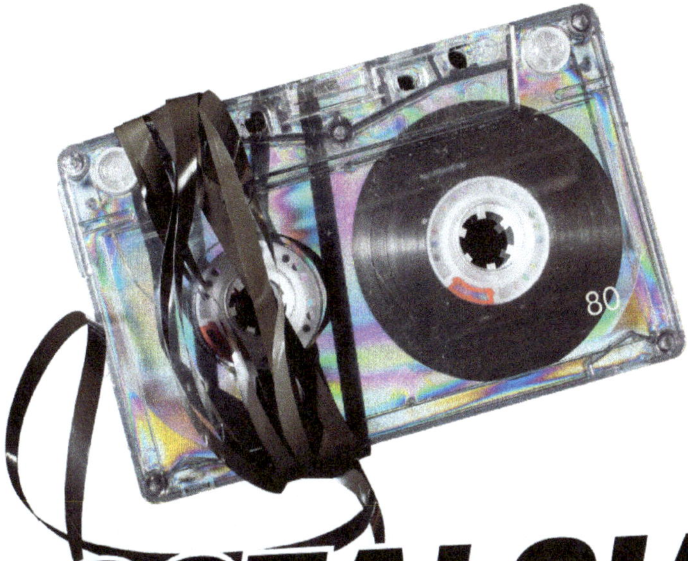

NOSTALGIA NATION

THE DEFINITIVE CHRONICLE OF
GROWING UP GEN X

JOHN TOMA
That 80s Dude

www.that80sdude.com

Copyright © 2025 by John Toma (That 80s Dude)

All rights reserved. No part of this publication may be reproduced, distributed, or transmitted in any form or by any means, including photocopying, recording, or other electronic or mechanical methods, without the prior written permission of the publisher, except with brief quotations embodied in critical reviews and certain other noncommercial uses permitted by copyright law.

DISCLAIMER:
The events, people, places, and experiences described in this book are recounted to the best of the author's memory and reflect the author's personal recollections. References to brands, people, products, television shows, movies, music, and other cultural touchstones, including images, are used for historical accuracy and context, and remain the property of their respective owners. Their inclusion does not imply endorsement of this work. This book represents the author's personal journey and interpretations of historical events.

FAIR USE NOTICE:
Any images, video stills, advertisements, song lyrics, catchphrases, and other copyrighted materials (if referenced) are reproduced strictly for historical documentation and cultural analysis under the fair use provisions of Section 107 of the U.S. Copyright Act. All images, logos, trademarks, and properties remain the property of their respective owners. Their inclusion is essential to chronicling this historical period, and no ownership is claimed.

Title: Nostalgia Nation: The Definitive Chronicle of Growing Up Gen X
Author: John Toma (That 80s Dude)

Published by Saint & Sentry | saintsentry.com
Book and Cover Design by Saint & Sentry
Printed in the United States on acid-free paper

For permissions or inquiries, please contact 80sDudeTV@gmail.com

Hardcover ISBN 979-8-9929532-3-7 (Dust Jacket HC, Color Int., IngramSpark)
Hardcover ISBN 979-8-9929532-2-0 (Coffee Table Special Edition, Color Int., Amazon)
Paperback ISBN 979-8-9929532-0-6 (BW Int., Amazon)
Ebook ISBN 979-8-9929532-1-3 (Color int., Live Links, Amazon)

First Edition (June 2025)

TO BETHANY —

My wife and best friend.
Thank you for your endless patience, boundless support, laughing with me, and sometimes at me. I am truly grateful for your love and encouragement.

TO MY PARENTS —

Thank you for your unwavering love, support, and belief in me. Your sacrifices have shaped my journey. Your blessing and encouragement mean everything to me.

Contents

FOREWARD	IX
PROLOGUE	XI
X | WHO IS GEN X?	XIII
1. Growing Up In The 80s	1
2. Get Back Home Before Dark	9
3. The Soundtrack of Our Youth	17
4. Hip Hop, Grunge, & Fashion	35
5. Dial-Up Daze	45
6. The Arcade Experience	57
7. The Games That Made Us	63
8. The Toys We Grew Up With	85
9. Enter The VHS	107
10. 80S & 90s Cinema	115
11. Prime-Time Nostalgia	125
12. The Golden Age of Sports?	157
13. RIP Saturday Morning Nostalgia	171
14. Sights, Sounds, and Feels	181
15. RIP Humanity... & American Neighborhoods	193
16. Trick-or-Treat Gen X Style	205
17. Days of Christmas Past	221

18. The Totally Real (and Totally Not) Fears of Our Youth	235
19. The Years That Made Us	243
20. The Future of Nostalgia	261
WHAT'S NEXT?	275
ACKNOWLEDGMENTS	277
ABOUT THE AUTHOR	279

FOREWARD

By Lisa Downs
Film Producer & Director

When John first asked me to write the forward to his incredible book, I mistakenly thought it would be a simple task. "Writing about nostalgia? Easy!" But as I sat down to get started, I realized how the words I wanted to say didn't come easy. The more I thought about it, the more I realized how much weight one simple word has. NOSTALGIA.

In one word, you have years of memories, of feelings, of hopes and dreams. You have memories of Saturday mornings, of adventures with friends, your first big screen film experience, hearing your favorite band for the first time... all the building blocks of who you are as a person today.

It's such a simple word to say, but it's a word that holds such an all encompassing, visceral wave of emotions for whoever thinks back on their own nostalgia.

I don't know at what point I began to look back on my childhood as years that I longed for, but as I get older, the more I find myself incorporating elements of my youth into what I do now. For the past 10 years my whole world has been nostalgia - not just through my "Life After..." films, but in my everyday life. The music I still listen to, the films I continue to watch, the VHS I continue to play, and the cassettes I still fix with a pencil.

Do we look back with rose coloured glasses? Maybe. But I wouldn't have it any other way.

To meet like-minded people such as *That 80s Dude* on this nostalgic journey is the icing on what is already a wonderful and magical cake, to keep hold of what defined me growing up. I am so lucky to have John as part of my documentaries, and I am so excited for people to read this incredible book, and see what shared memories unfold on the pages.

PROLOGUE

Nostalgia Matters

It's a warm summer day 1980-something and I'm sprawled out on the shag carpet in my family's living room, staring up at the TV screen. The opening credits of *The A-Team* are rolling, and I'm filled with excitement and anticipation. For the next hour, I'll be transported into a world of action, adventure, and improbable heroics. As the show unfolds, I'll cheer on my favorite characters, marvel at their exploits, and soak in the catchy theme song that will be stuck in my head for years to come.

On my *The Real Ghostbusters* lap tray sits a plate of SPAM mixed in with scrambled eggs, a signature dish my mom would throw together to hold me over for a little while. Somewhere in the home, between wooden brown walls, I can hear my sisters screaming at each other because one of them didn't ask the other if she could borrow her blouse. My eyes float to the blinking clock on our VCR my dad got from a flea market and they settle on the spine label of a bootleg recording of Conan The Barbarian. *That will be tonight's movie after everyone is in bed*, I think to myself.

Fast forward to today, and here I am, perched in front of my laptop, delving into the cultural phenomenon of nostalgia while occasionally checking Instagram to catch up with my favorite creators — many of whom have become friends and integral parts of my online community. After doling out likes and comments, I anxiously check my latest post's performance. A flood of likes and shares? YES! With my nostalgia-induced dopamine hit secured, I dive back into my research, and it becomes crystal clear: I'm far from alone in my affection for the past. Across generations, people are seeking comfort in the familiar as they navigate the complexities of modern life. It's evident in the resurgence of 80s and 90s fashion, the revival of classic tunes, and the wild popularity of rebooted TV shows and movies. Our shared longing for the past is more than just a trend. The power of nostalgia is undeniable, offering a comforting refuge in a world that has become increasingly uncomfortable and uncertain for many. The past's magnetic pull stirs a peculiar longing in us. We seem to yearn for moments we can't reclaim. The urge to share childhood treasures with strangers, the unexpected nostalgia for once-ignored commercials, the deep desire to connect with others who remember these shared experiences — these behaviors reveal something profound. Behind this collective reminiscence lies a deeper question: why do fragments of our past hold such power over our present?

These questions, and many more, drove me to write this book. Through personal anecdotes and cultural analysis, I'll be exploring the various ways that nostalgia is shaping our lives and our society. I'll delve into the psychological and cultural reasons behind our nostalgia, and examine the different paths other content creators have found to fill the void so many of us are feeling today, and why we've embraced this outlet of escape.

MOSTLY, WE'RE GOING TO HAVE A BLAST TRAVELING BACK IN TIME TO RELIVE SOME OF THE GREATEST MOMENTS OF OUR YOUTH!

For you youngsters — I'm giving you a front-row seat to what it was really like growing up Gen X. Maybe you'll glimpse why your parents (or grandparents - ouch) are the way we are. And since you're already deep into your own nostalgia game, consider this a heads-up: document everything, save those precious bits of your youth. Trust me, those "worthless" toys and memories? They're pieces of your story that'll mean more than you can imagine right now.

Besides inspiring you, I hope this book makes you laugh and reminisce about the days we look back on with great fondness and pride.

Thank you for reading, and if you love it, and agree that *nostalgia matters*, please make sure you subscribe to my newsletter. Visit www.that80sdude.com

Stay Rad!

John

Ps. *For the best, most immersive experience—including full-color photos—be sure to check out the eBook as a perfect complement to this print edition!*

X | WHO IS GEN X?

Hands down, the coolest and most significant generation around today is Generation X. We are the generation that won't dismiss the immense hardships and sacrifices made by previous generations because we directly inherited their wisdom, values, patriotism, and stories firsthand, before technology reshaped how history is shared and remembered. We sat at kitchen tables with grandparents who survived the Great Depression and fought in World War II, listening intently to their experiences while our Boomer parents worked late hours to provide for us. These moments shaped us into keen observers and natural historians. To that point, we are also the only generation that won't dismiss history.

We are the old guard and the bridge generation—the last to remember a world without smartphones and social media, yet we ushered in the digital age and founded influential tech companies like Google, Amazon, eBay, PayPal, YouTube, and Wikipedia.

As latchkey kids, we came home to empty houses with keys dangling from yarn around our necks, making our own snacks, and learning independence by necessity. We didn't have playdates or helicopter parents—we had neighborhood friends and we made our own adventure. We rode our bikes until the streetlights came on, solved our own problems, and developed a resilience that would serve us well in the decades to come.

We also bridged the analog and digital divide. We went from vinyl to 8-track to cassette to CD to MP3, and we appreciated every evolution. A lot of us still hold on to these items. We were the last generation to use card catalogs in libraries, yet we built Google. We grew up with three TV channels but created YouTube. We remember busy signals and payphones, yet we pioneered remote work culture. This unique perspective gives us an almost supernatural ability to adapt to change while maintaining a healthy skepticism about each "next big thing."

Generation X mastered the art of self-reliance while nurturing a deep appreciation for community. We created our own entertainment, made mix tapes, played pocket games (with those little metal balls), and mastered Nintendo games. Our music—from new wave to grunge to hip-hop—broke boundaries and gave voice to universal frustrations and hopes. Our movies and TV shows continue to be admired and copied today.

We are the generation that perfected the eye-roll, mastered irony as an art form, and turned skepticism into a superpower. Yet, beneath our sardonic exterior lies a deep well of compassion and pragmatism. We witnessed significant historical events, from watching the Challenger explosion live in our classrooms to seeing the Berlin Wall fall and experiencing both the rise and decline of the MTV era. Each moment taught us to question authority while seeking truth and to rebel against convention while striving to create something better.

We navigated multiple recessions, adapted to countless technological revolutions, and emerged with our sense of humor intact. While the media may have labeled us as slackers, we were actually busy innovating, creating, and reimagining what work could be.

As parents, we've struck a unique balance, rejecting both the hands-off approach we grew up with and the helicopter parenting that followed. We teach our kids the value of independence while remaining engaged and supportive. We want them to have the freedom we had, but with the safety net we sometimes wished for.

Now, as we navigate the complexities of middle age, Generation X continues to serve as cultural translators. We explain TikTok to Boomers and vinyl records to Gen Z. We appreciate both handwritten letters and instant messages. We understand the value of traditional wisdom and the necessity of innovation. We're equally comfortable with actual face time and FaceTime.

Our generation doesn't seek the spotlight — we're too busy getting things done. We're the ones keeping businesses running, raising families, caring for aging parents, and still finding time to perfect our playlists—and running social media accounts on the side!

We're not interested in generational warfare because we've learned that every generation has something valuable to offer.

Generation X may be smaller in numbers than the generations that bookend us, but our impact has been profound and far-reaching. We are the custodians of the past and the architects of the future, the generation that remembers what was while building what could be. In a world of increasing polarization, we remain the bridge builders, the mediators, the ones who can see both sides while charting a path forward.

This is Generation X. We are undiluted, unfiltered, and unapologetically authentic. We're still here, still adapting, still innovating, and still keeping it realer than anyone else. And we're just getting started.

Oh, and we were born between 1965 and 1980.

Important 1980s Magazine Issues From My Personal Collection

"If my calculations are correct, when this baby hits 88 miles per hour, you're going to see some serious sh-t."

Doc Brown
(Back To The Future - 1985)

Chapter One

Growing Up In The 80s

WHAT IT WAS REALLY LIKE

What was it really like growing up in the 80s? I get this question a lot. There is a fascination with growing up in the 80s, and you may find this shocking, but a lot of "younger" folks have become so intrigued by the decade because of all the superhero films and streaming shows that pay homage to that time (*Stranger Things* being one such show, and *Cobra Kai* being another), that they're actually part of a growing creator segment building fan pages celebrating the 80s and 90s.

The years between 1980 and 1995 brought about significant changes to everyday life, and I'm not just talking about the enhanced Taco Bell menu and decor. Back when I was in third grade, around 1982, we only had a handful of television channels. If there was nothing good on, tough luck. There was no cable TV or streaming like it exists today, and we didn't get our first VCR until the mid-80s. They were very expensive! So, if we missed a movie in the theater, we had to wait until it aired on TV, which might take forever. It was always a thrill when classic films like *The Wizard of Oz* or *The Sound of Music* broadcast annually during the holidays. We could look forward to seeing the Rankin/Bass Claymation specials and the Charlie Brown cartoons.

We eventually moved to Oak Park, MI and rented a home that actually had a microwave. My mom never used it though because she said it would give us cancer. So it just sat there. Admittedly, I used it a few times to cook frozen dinners without her knowledge. Sorry mom.

We also got cable television, which introduced me to MTV, a must-have for any 80s kid. Before we got cable, I mostly watched entertainment at a cousin's or neighbor's house. If you had cable tv during those days, your home was everyone's entertainment spot!

RAD FACT: It wasn't until 1988 that over 50% of households had cable tv!

When we finally got a cordless phone, it felt like a luxury to be able to talk on the phone outside of the kitchen. I can't remember having a cordless phone until around 1989. We were chorded and landlocked throughout the 1980s.

For school projects, we turned to the Encyclopedia Britannica or headed to the local library, and if that didn't work, we asked our dad, who we assumed knew everything. He did not.

Although all of this may sound archaic to the younger generation, it was a simpler time, and as children, we enjoyed far more freedom. Without technology to keep us indoors, we spent our days outside, roaming the neighborhood all summer long. There were no cell phones, so if we wanted to stay at a friend's house for dinner, we simply had their parents call ours. If we wanted to hang out the following day, we made commitments before we went inside for dinner.

Riding bikes without helmets, playing in the rain, and spending hours building forts were a few of our favorite pastimes. If it was hot enough to cook eggs on the street, we all met up at the fire hydrant mid-day for a neighborhood water event. An adult would remove the cap and crank the valve open, and we would be the happiest kids in the world.

Things weren't all sunshine and rainbows.

Detroit in the 80s was something else. It was gritty and dangerous. There were rules. Street rules. When someone my age says we grew up fast, we mean it. That's the reality of growing up in a tough environment. It's a mix of what you learn at home and what you experience on the streets. Even as a kid, I knew which areas to avoid at certain times. There were people you could trust, people you couldn't, and then there were the "crazies." You never wanted to run into them.

We meticulously planned our adventures exploring the many abandoned homes near State Fair and 7-Mile Road. This was essential because some of these locations were near drug dealer corners and gang alleys, areas that were notoriously dangerous even during daylight hours. While exploring these abandoned homes was thrilling, we were always mindful of the potential risks. We never knew who or what might be lurking inside, seeking temporary shelter. The structural integrity of these buildings was often questionable, adding another layer of danger to our explorations. Remember those pictures of missing kids on milk cartons? Yeah, that really messed with us. We were constantly hearing scary stories about kidnappings and kids being forced to take drugs. While we enjoyed a sense of freedom, we also had to face some frightening realities.

Sometimes, we had leftover M-80 firecrackers from the 4th of July. We brought them along on our adventures, just in case we wanted to add a little excitement to those empty houses. Or, if we needed a quick escape from "the crazies" – or even if we just pretended we did. Looking back, it's pretty incredible to think that even potential danger didn't deter us from our explorations.

On rainy days, we would play board games like Monopoly, Hotels, Solar Quest, Hungry Hungry Hippos, Mouse Trap, or Operation, just to name a few. More often than not, we'd just sit on the porch and watch the storm and think about all the fun we were going to have when the rain cleared. We listened to music, wrote our own stories, sorted our baseball cards, read comic books, browsed the TV Guide and memorized the Saturday morning cartoon schedule. I used to spend so much time making my own mixtapes on the hand-me-down boombox we had. Sometimes we went outside to play and ride our bikes in the puddles. We built make-shift and dangerous ramps to jump those puddles. Sometimes we landed the jumps, and other times we didn't and we returned home with cuts and scrapes.

I'm often asked why I feel so strongly that there will never be another time like the 80s again. I think the best way to describe it is with this analogy.

Let's say the 80s are like a 2-liter soda bottle you just bought. As you twist open the cap, there's a satisfying hiss that fills the air, like the whisper of a thousand tiny bubbles coming to life. The bubbles race to the surface, and the aroma of sweet, tantalizing flavor envelops you. You take a drink and that first sip is exhilarating. The fizz tickles your tongue, and it's a moment of pure bliss. But here's the thing. As the soda bottle sits out, the lively fizz gradually fades, leaving behind a stillness that echoes the passing of time. The bubbles, once vibrant and full of life, now settle into a quiet resignation. The soda's once invigorating flavor grows dull, losing its edge and sinking into a flat, subdued sweetness. But that sweetness is deceiving, and now replaced by a mellow, lackluster taste. The vibrant spirit of the soda has slipped away, leaving only a memory of the effervescent joy it once brought. Similarly, each decade after the 80s has been a slow deterioration of the brightness and fullness we once lived through. I bet you if you asked a 90s kid if this is true, they would agree. There was still fizz and verve in the nineties. The flavor faded in the late 2000s and if I had to pinpoint an exact moment, it would be June 29, 2007. The smartphone ushered in the false sweetness this generation has come to know, and is just now coming to grips with.

Yes, the 80s were truly wonderful, and I believe being a kid in the 1980s made them more wonderful. Although there were hardships and adversity, there was the sort of freedom and hope you clung to, and your neighbors looked out for you. I've spoken to so many from my generation and the consensus is that we took so many things for granted back then, having no idea how drastically things would change over the years. We were just living in the moment.

Today, my generation watches with amazement how the vast web of connectivity somehow continues to diminish genuine connections between members of society. This is why we feel cautious about the pace and impact of technology.

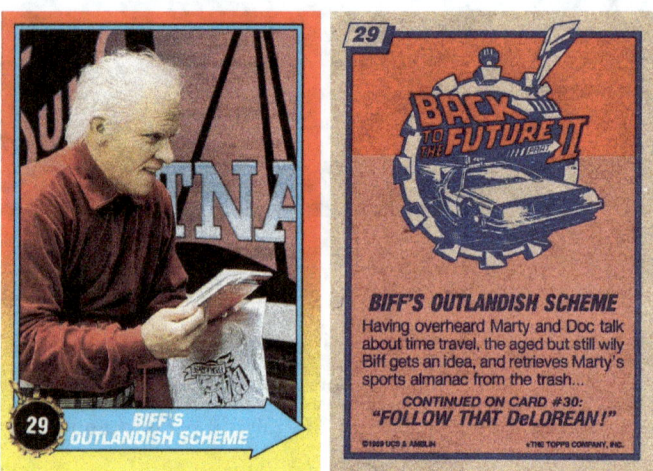

Back To The Future II Trading Cards | Topps

I remember watching *Back To The Future II* when I was a kid, and it instilled in me this sense of wonder about what the future was really going to look like. I think we were all excited about one day having hoverboards, flying cars, and self-lacing shoes. There was going to be progress. And despite the futuristic setting, the movie emphasized timeless values such as the importance of family, relationships, and staying true to one's principles.

However, the plot of *BTTF II* also emphasizes how actions taken in the past can have unforeseen and often negative consequences in the future (Biff's use of the sports almanac). While we have undoubtedly made progress, we have also sacrificed simplicity and embraced a false sense of connection, leaving us to question whether our advancements are truly beneficial, or if they've come at too high a price.

"At some point in your childhood, you and your friends went outside to play together for the last time, and nobody knew it."

Unknown

Chapter Two

Get Back Home Before Dark

One of the most significant differences between then and now was the freedom we had to play outside and explore our neighborhoods. Our parents didn't hover over us or worry if we were gone all day, as long as we came back when the streetlights came on. This way of living was common all over the country. I can't honestly say that's the case today.

As a grown man living in a far different world than in the 80s and 90s, I'm not naïve to the fact there were child abductions and other crimes that happened in those days. Even as a kid, I knew this. I disliked looking at the back of milk cartons because I didn't want to see who was missing. I looked anyway, because I knew it was a reality.

I can still vividly remember the public service announcement, "It's 10PM, Do you know where your children are?" Can you imagine something like this being aired on television today?

1980s Public Service Announcement

Every Gen X kid will admit their unease when they heard the opening intro to *America's Most Wanted*, the television show hosted by John Walsh.

Walsh became an anti-crime activist following the kidnapping and murder of his son, Adam, in 1981.

America's Most Wanted TV guide Print Ad - John Walsh

We got seriously freaked out by the show's opening. As if that wasn't enough, *Unsolved Mysteries* just piled on the nightmare fuel.

Maybe this was all something that helped me in my career later in life; training security personnel around the country on drug recognition and narcotics detection. The stories I heard from probationers and parolees are enough to write a book.

But when you're a kid, especially back then, you just did whatever you wanted, and threw caution to the wind.

'Unsolved Mysteries' LIVE! Print Ad (NBC Primetime, November 25, 1992)

For me personally, growing up in 1980s Detroit, playing outside was the ultimate freedom. It was truly visceral. Just imagine what it was like going out each day, unsure of who you were going to run into while adventuring. There were certainly people and places we knew to keep away from, and this was what helped us create deeper bonds with our neighborhood friends.

***

It was nineteen-eighty-something, and we were riding past the local liquor store heading home for the day. The light was fading quickly and the street lights were warming up to their steady glow. This meant we were risking two things, getting home before dark, and missing a warm meal.

But there he was. POPS, the neighborhood boogeyman and gangster that was notorious for popping out of alleyways. This was *Seven Mile & Bauman*, and POPS ran these streets.

Seven Mile & Bauman (The Repair and Tire Shop on the right was my uncle's from 1980 to approx. the mid-2000s)

I was always told you should never look him in the eyes. The kids around the neighborhood would tell stories of running into POPS. Many stories ended with, *"...and that kid was never seen again."*

POPS always fascinated me, so I looked right into his eyes that day. He got a good look at each of us because we just froze. He seemed to recognize us as kids from the neighborhood, so he walked right past us into the liquor store. Coincidentally, or maybe not, that same liquor store had POPS spray painted on its exterior. We sped off when he disappeared into the liquor store. The next time I saw POPS was on my grandmother's street nearby, where he demanded that a man not stab another with a kitchen knife right in front of me on her neighbor's lawn. But that's another story.

This sort of stuff was not uncommon in Detroit. There was regular talk of someone being killed at a gas station, or kids being robbed at gunpoint, and their bikes and shoes being taken. Our parents reminded us to be aware of our surroundings.

E. Detroit/Van Dyke, 7-Mile Rd

Despite some of the real world fear that existed, we had a blast and lived in the moment. If you're reading this, you probably remember opening fire hydrants and running through the stream of water to cool off in the hot summers. You likely also recall the dangerous ramps we built for jumping our bikes - the thrill of danger made it even more exciting. The playgrounds of our youth were often constructed of rusted metal and concrete, and the risk of injury only added to the sense of adventure. If you haven't been thrown from a merry-go-round, have you truly lived?

While roaming the neighborhood with friends, we used our imaginations to create fun games and reenactments from tv shows or movies we had seen. We played tag, hide-and-seek, and capture-the-flag until the sun went down. We would bring our toys out to the front lawns and dig holes into the grass to create moats and tiny forts for our G.I. Joe and Masters of The Universe action figures. I remember playing marbles, and losing a lot of them in bets we made, but also winning a lot of them. It was a time when children could be children, and although the world was dangerous, our parents just didn't seem to worry too much about us being outside all day... as long as we were back by dinner.

Looking back, it's amazing to think about the freedom we had and the adventures we went on. I think about my kids now and how they rarely ever experience these things with the neighbor's kids. After the pandemic, you could forget about kids interacting face to face.

I truly feel for the kids of today. During our time, even without cell phones, we still figured out how to connect with our friends and find things to do together. Yes, I will be the first to admit we spent hours playing Nintendo or Sega, but we escaped outside still and went to one another's homes and hung out. Our imaginations and the world outside our front doors were enough to keep us occupied and happy for hours on end. I can't tell you how often I wish this for kids today. Technology, while it connects this younger generation to the world through gaming and apps, is temporary and impersonal in so many ways. It's been sold to the younger generation as the ultimate connector, and in some ways it is, but the connections are fleeting and often impersonal.

While rare, there are still some small communities in the United States that maintain a simpler lifestyle. In these places, children can play freely outside, and neighbors look out for each other. Unfortunately, these close-knit communities are becoming increasingly scarce.

Will there ever be a resurgence of these simpler times, where kids are told to be back before it's dark? I truly hope so.

The street lights have to warm up to their steady glow somewhere.

Abandoned Detroit Neighborhood

"You know, Andie... They just don't write love songs like they used to."

Duckie Dale
(Pretty In Pink - 1986)

Chapter Three

The Soundtrack of Our Youth

The Music That Defines Growing Up Gen X

The thirteen most quintessential songs of the 80s and 90s are (drum roll) — Before we dive into the songs, let's lay the groundwork first.

Staying Power

Everyone knows 80s music is the best music. If they don't, get rid of them. You don't need that kind of negativity in your life!

80s music is so unique and memorable that it continues to have a powerful presence in today's media. You can still hear it in current movie soundtracks, commercials, sporting events, and even video games!

Why is that? Why has the music previous to the 1980s not affected culture as profoundly as 80 music has today?

Step Brothers (2008) | Sony Pictures

We can all agree that 80s music was pure fun. Let's compare it to the second best decade for music, the 1990s. While 90s music is special, and incredible bands were still emerging, music was changing. It was moodier, scratchier, and I'd say there were more bands that were an acquired taste. Still, the 90s was an incredible decade for music. I mean, no one can deny that 90s R&B was absolute magic. Oh, and let's not forget, Freestyle Music!

RAD FACTS:

1. **The Birthplace of Freestyle** ~ Freestyle originated in **New York City**, particularly in the Bronx, during the early 1980s. It was heavily influenced by Latin disco, hip-hop, and electro-funk, reflecting the multicultural blend of the city at the time.

2. **The Role of DJs and Producers** ~ Pioneering DJs like **Jellybean Benitez** and producers such as **Arthur Baker** and **Tony Moran** were instrumental in shaping the sound. They used drum machines like the Roland TR-808 and synthesizers like the Yamaha DX7 to create its signature electronic beats.

3. **The First Freestyle Hit** ~ *Let the Music Play* by Shannon, released in 1983, is widely considered the first major Freestyle hit. The song's innovative sound bridged the gap between post-disco and dance-pop, becoming a global sensation.

4. **Latin Roots** ~ Freestyle music was dominated by artists of Puerto Rican,

Cuban, and other Latin-American backgrounds. Performers like **Lisa Lisa and Cult Jam**, **TKA**, **Debby Deb**, and **Exposé** brought Latin flavor to mainstream dance music.

5. **The Decline and Revival** ~ Freestyle's popularity declined in the mid-90s as house music, grunge, and hip-hop rose to prominence. However, it experienced a revival in the 2000s and continues to thrive in niche communities and nostalgic events.

With its lighthearted feel, 1980s music reflected the trends of the time, much like the movies of the decade with their unique aesthetic. The Yamaha DX7 keyboard played a key role in shaping that iconic 80s sound. I believe our music's enduring appeal goes beyond just the innovative synthesizer sounds. Its popularity stemmed from its innovative nature, engaging programming like MTV, and a wide range of genres that appealed to diverse audiences. These things all worked together to make the music and the musicians more memorable.

Yamaha DX-7

It's also worth noting, and I'd be remiss not to mention, that even our 80s and 90s cartoons featured amazing music and talent. I mean, the intro to Jayce and The Wheeled Warriors proves our music was just on a different level.

For those of us that grew up in the 80s, the music of that decade was a constant presence in our lives. It was a stark contrast to the music our parents listened to, creating a clear generational divide. Our parents had their iconic bands like The Beatles and Rolling Stones, but we found our voice in the sounds of Tears for Fears and Guns N' Roses. This new wave of music was our form of rebellion, and ultimately, it became a defining part of our identity.

Much of today's music simply doesn't appeal to me. I realize I probably sound like an old-timer when I say that!

While there's still some wonderful music being produced today, it's rare. Most contemporary music feels amateurish and doesn't leave a lasting impression. It's hard to imagine any current bands achieving the same longevity as those from our generation. Although there are a few exceptionally talented solo artists today, they're often overshadowed by the sheer volume of mediocre music.

***

MTV airs for the first time on August 1, 1981

I WANT MY MTV

Remember how much MTV changed the world of music? It changed cultural awareness of music and blending music with film. Unlike Spotify, which revolutionized music delivery, MTV's impact was far more profound. It wasn't just a platform; it became an integral part of our lives. While Spotify's execution was superior, even to Apple's, MTV's groundbreaking influence was undeniable.

Before MTV, the only way to experience our favorite tunes was live in person or on the radio. But MTV changed everything! We could now spend most of our day watching music videos and seeing our favorite artists perform. Every week brought new and innovative videos. We were introduced to new music genres like new wave, synthpop, and hair metal, and we couldn't get enough!

MTV brought us closer to the bands we loved, and it also made learning about music much more fun. I loved watching the VJs interview bands and music artists. I also ate up all the drama.

Do you remember when MTV News was just getting started? It was pretty basic back then. Every hour, you'd see that MTV News logo pop up behind the VJ, and they'd give you a quick rundown of what was happening in the music scene. We're talking maybe two and a half minutes, tops. The VJ would tell us about new albums dropping, artists announcing tours or which ones trashed their hotel room, or give us a sneak peek at a video shoot. It was short, simple, and just enough information to keep us in the loop about what was going on in the music world. I loved it!

RAD FACT:

MTV's iconic logo, featuring the large "M" with "TV" spray-painted on it, was designed by Manhattan Design in late 1980, just before MTV launched in 1981. Manhattan Design's work with MTV catapulted them into the spotlight, making them the go-to designers for avant-garde projects in the music industry. Their client list soon read like a who's who of 80s pop and rock, featuring iconic acts such as The B-52s, The Cars, Billy Idol, Duran Duran, and R.E.M. They also lent their distinctive style to projects for Sting, 10,000 Maniacs, and Suzanne Vega, among others. Their association with MTV had effectively established them as the designers of choice for anyone looking to capture that coveted "hip" aesthetic of the era.

One of the most memorable aspects of 80s music was the larger-than-life rock stars who seemed to live on the edge. Bands like Guns N' Roses, Def Leppard, and Motley Crue were notorious for their wild antics and their hard-partying lifestyles. It was a time when musicians could get away with almost anything, and as fans, we absolutely loved it!

We also had pop icons like Michael Jackson, Madonna, and Prince, who were changing the face of music with their unique styles and sounds. They all influenced fashion as well. Remember Madonna's bold fashion statements, especially the outfits she wore during her live performances? What about Michael Jackson's iconic red leather jacket?

The Wedding Singer (1998) from New Line Cinema

Artists from the 80s undoubtedly served as a major source of inspiration for future musicians and bands, particularly in terms of fashion.

***

THE UK INFLUENCE

While American acts dominated much of the 80s music scene, we can't overlook the massive impact of British bands that rocked our world and made their mark on American music culture. Groups like Def Leppard, with their arena rock anthems, and Duran Duran, with their catchy new wave pop, absolutely took over in the US.

Back in 1989, I worked as an apprentice at a place called Classic Sounds, where we installed custom audio systems in cars. One of my favorite things to do on the weekends, during my lunch, was to sit inside the "demo room" and listen to music while eating my sandwich and drinking Snapple. There was one cassette in particular I listened to all the time and that was the album, *Synchronicity*, by The Police. I'm a super-fan of The Police.

I've always loved how they blended rock, reggae, and pop to create one of the most unique sounds in music.

Read the article at that80s dude.com

Then, there was New Order, *which* emerged from the ashes of Joy Division to pioneer the fusion of post-punk and electronic dance music. The first time I heard *Bizzare Love Triangle,* their sound absolutely blew me away!

A few other of my favorite UK groups included The Cure, Depeche Mode, and *The Smiths*.

Interestingly, the term *New Wave* itself originated in the UK music press of the late 1970s to market punk-related styles without using the word *punk*, which had gained negative connotations. By the early 80s, this term had crossed the Atlantic and become a catch-all for various post-punk and synth-pop styles, showcasing how British music trends were shaping the global scene.

I'm mostly an 80s New Wave fan. I was not that into the 90s *Britpop* invasion. However, there were a few bands that stood out to me I listened to regularly. Bands like Oasis, Blur, Pulp, and Suede, brought a distinctly British flavor to their rock music, and it was easy to listen to. These bands had catchy melodies and lyrics often steeped in British culture and slang.

Do you recall the rivalry between Oasis and Blur? Remember when both bands released singles on the same day, August 14, 1995?! I remember reading headlines titled *Battle of Britpop*!

Yes, The Spice Girls took over for a while, and that was fun, especially the David Beckham and Posh Spice years, but the Britpop bubble eventually burst towards the end of the decade. Still, we were introduced to bands like Radiohead, The Verve, Placebo, Snow Patrol, and Coldplay. Without a doubt, 90s Britpop was, and still is, significant.

As you can see, MTV was certainly a force for good. Without MTV, we may not have been introduced to some of our favorite bands. MTV played a huge role in making these international artists into global superstars.

I remember watching MTV music videos all day long on some weekends. Some of my favorite broadcast memories were when they introduced us to VJs like Martha Quinn, Downtown Julie Brown, Nina Blackwood, and Adam Curry. Also, thanks to MTV, these people became household names.

RAD FACT:

MTV coined the term "VJ" (video jockey) as a play on the radio term "DJ" (disc jockey). The original five VJs – **Nina Blackwood, Mark Goodman, Alan Hunter, J.J. Jackson**, and **Martha Quinn** – became celebrities in their own right, hosting specials and appearing in commercials.

Besides the music videos, MTV had shows like *Headbanger's Ball* and *Yo! MTV Raps*, which catered to fans of metal and hip hop, respectively. The channel also hosted events like *MTV Spring Break* and *MTV Video Music Awards*, which I watched through the early 2000s.

No one can dispute that by the time the late 90s came along, MTV had become something entirely different. It had lost its way. But had they? MTV has gotten a bad rap for going from playing music videos all day to moving into reality tv and other programming. What most people don't realize is that peak MTV was early to mid-early 1980s. The channel experienced a significant decline in ratings as the novelty of music videos wore off by the late 1980s. Some won't be happy to hear this, but *The Real World* actually revitalized MTV's viewership!

Sadly, in June 2024, twenty-five years of MTV music news disappeared from the internet thanks to Paramount, the parent company that holds MTV as an asset. It's a shame that a company would eliminate a cherished part of our history only to improve its bottom line.

Looking back on the music of the 80s and 90s, it's easy to see why people still love the music today. The younger generation has fallen in love with it too. There are so many social media accounts run by under-thirty creators that share music media from those two decades. Prices for vinyl, cassette, and CDs have been on the rise.

The fact is, the 80s and the 90s were a time when music felt important enough to discuss at school with our friends. We could escape into the world of music videos and knew great detail about our favorite rock stars.

My sixteen-year-old son and I frequently discuss music. He tells me that at his high school, students don't really talk about bands or music. They're more interested in discussing influencers. He discovers music primarily through Spotify or recommendations from me. This leads me to believe that this generation may not have the same level of passion for music as we did. However, I can't really blame them.

***

THE WALKMAN GENERATION

I can't talk about music and not mention the Sony Walkman and the art of making mixtapes. If you still embrace cassette culture, I salute you.

We witnessed some incredible advancements in technology in the 80s and The Nineties that changed the way we listened to music. I can't help but feel nostalgic about the days of cassette tapes and Walkman players. Back then, it was all about making mixtapes for ourselves and our friends, and carrying our music with us wherever we went. The Walkman was a game-changer, allowing us to listen to our music on the go, without having to carry around a bulky stereo system. And let's not forget the portable CD players that came later - they were a status symbol, and we would proudly show off our shiny new gadget to anyone who would listen. I remember if we really wanted to get crazy, we would set the mode to "Mega Bass."

***

MUSIC IN MY FIRST RIDE

Freedom smelled like leather seats and Armor All in the summer of '95. My chariot? A 1985 Chevy Camaro Berlinetta— all angles and attitude, purchased with two years worth of minimum wage savings and a prayer that the transmission wouldn't drop out on the test drive. I'd dreamed about the day I could get around on my own in a car that was uniquely me. It was independence wrapped in metal and an interior "so 80s" it would make you smile from ear to ear.

The Berlinetta was Chevy's attempt at making a "luxury" Camaro, which is like putting a tuxedo on a wrestler. It had these ridiculously futuristic digital gauges that worked about 60% of the time, and a steering wheel that looked like it belonged in Knight Rider. I rocked a Casio Data Bank watch, so you better believe I played Michael Knight whenever I got in!

The previous owner had installed a Pioneer stereo that I promptly connected to my Sony Discman via one of those cassette adapters that somehow survived being ejected a thousand times.

Now picture this: cruising down *Mission Blvd.*, windows rolled down, hair whipping in the wind, while carefully holding the Discman steady on the passenger seat to prevent it from skipping. One pothole and Guns N' Roses would stutter like Max Headroom. The solution? An elaborate system of foam cushion padding glued inside a custom box I made so I could access the Discman buttons easily, creating the world's most sophisticated shock absorption system. In hind-sight, I should have patented that concept!

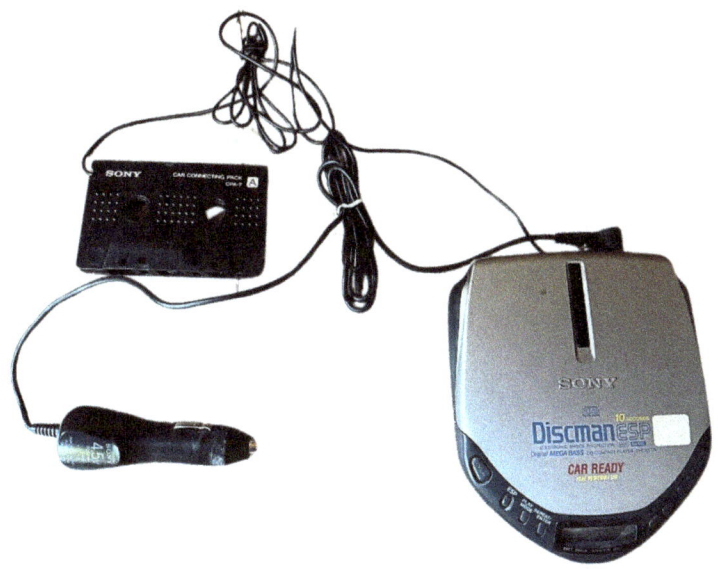

My '85 Camaro had personality quirks that would make a therapist rich. The power windows operated on their own mysterious schedule. The driver's seat had a sweet spot that, once found, you never adjusted for fear of breaking whatever precarious balance kept it functional. And don't get me started on the digital dash display that occasionally went full disco light show for no apparent reason.

But man, when that 305 V8 roared to life, none of that mattered. Every time I turned the key, it felt like the opening credits of my own movie. The Berlinetta might not have been the fastest Camaro ever built— it was more highway cruiser than street racer— but try telling that to my 18-year-old self, burning through gas money I couldn't afford, living for those Friday night cruises by the beach.

My mobile music collection lived in those zip-up CD cases, packed with carefully curated mix CDs labeled with Sharpie artwork. The case rode shotgun like a loyal companion, ready to provide the perfect soundtrack for any mood or misadventure.

Looking back, I experienced glorious moments because of the freedom that Camaro provided me. One night, while out with my girlfriend, I parked along the east side of Mission Bay beach in San Diego (*Mission Point Park*). Let's just say that I also experienced glorious moments inside my Camaro. We were out so late that night that we were locked inside the parking lot. I had to knock on beach resident doors until I found one that let me use their phone to call a friend. My best friend came to pick us up so I could get my girlfriend back home. That experience will always be imprinted in my mind, because he showed up in HIS first car, a Toyota MR2. We somehow fit in the passenger seat. She had to ride on my lap the entire forty-minute ride home. But what a night it was!

Sure, my Camaro drank gas like a fish, the A/C was more theoretical than functional, and it had more rattles than a newborn's toy. But it was mine. Every oil stain on the driveway, every mysterious noise that I turned up the music to drown out, every late-night cruise with nowhere particular to go - it was all part of the story.

Sometimes I wonder if kids today get the same feeling from their first cars. There's something special about a vehicle that's old enough to have a personality, young enough to still run, and just unreliable enough to teach you basic mechanics whether you wanted to learn them or not. My '85 Camaro was a life coach with a V8 engine, flashy interior, and an attitude problem. It was also where my music came along with me and each drive had its own soundtrack.

I sold it three years later when I blew out the transmission a second time racing it. I just couldn't afford all the work I was putting into it, but I regret not holding on to that car. I drive a Jeep today, and on certain nights when I'm cruisin' and the stars align, I swear I can still hear that Camaro engine rumble, usually right when I start a Pearl Jam track. My

'85 Camaro might be long gone, but the memories, freedom, youth, and questionable mechanical decisions will always live on.

Making mixtapes was an art form, and we took it seriously. We would spend hours recording songs onto blank cassettes, pausing and unpausing the tape at just the right moment to create seamless transitions between tracks. And there was no way we were going to give a mixtape to anyone without decorating it and adding our personal touch! No way!

Well, except for that one time I gave an all black mixtape to this goth girl I was sort of crushin' on in first year band class - even used rubbing alcohol to remove the gold title lines from both A and B sides. But, I suppose one could argue that's a decorative choice I made.

Not everything was about personal music devices. Music radio was also a way of life for Gen X kids. We would tune into our favorite stations and listen to the latest hits, eagerly waiting for our favorite songs to come on. Casey Kasem and his *Top 40 Countdown* were a weekly event that we would look forward to, waiting to see which songs would make the top 40 cut.

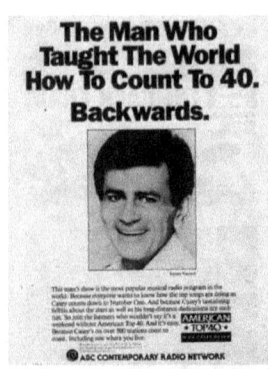
Casey Kasem Top 40 Ad

Looking back on those days, it's hard not to laugh at how much effort we put into something as simple as listening to music.

Do we take music for granted today because of convenient tech? I think we do. The tactile experience that required us to spend time and make an effort to listen to music, and even required us to wait patiently until the song actually played on the radio, made the experience far more intimate.

***

THE IMPORTANCE OF 80S MUSIC TODAY

Eighties music pulses through our cultural DNA, its synthesizers and power chords echoing decades later. These weren't just songs playing in the background–they were witnesses to first kisses in parked cars, companions through teenage heartbreak, anthems blasting at house parties when our parents were away. Today, watching teenagers discover Depeche Mode and The Cure feels like a strange validation. Our music didn't just survive; it flourished, finding new life in corners of the world we never imagined, speaking to kids who weren't even born when these tracks first crackled over FM radio.

Today, 80s music continues to influence modern artists, with many sampling or covering classic 80s tracks. The resurgence of synth-pop and the ongoing popularity of 80s-inspired shows like *Stranger Things* have introduced a whole new generation to the sounds of our youth.

The 80s were a time of significant social and political change, and the music reflected that. From protest songs to anthems of individuality, 80s music taught us to question authority, express ourselves, embrace our uniqueness, and defy societal expectations. These lessons remain relevant today, which is perhaps why younger generations find such resonance in these decades-old tracks.

For Gen X kids, 80s music will always be special because it represents a time when music felt personal and powerful. In an age of streaming and algorithms, there's something to be said for the shared experience of waiting for your favorite song on the radio or staying up late to catch a music video premiere on MTV.

Alright, let's get down to the nitty-gritty: the thirteen most quintessential songs of the 1980s — I'm talking the songs that'll take any Gen X kid straight back to the best decade ever.

- "Like a Virgin" by Madonna (1984)
- "Take On Me" by a-ha (1985)
- "Don't Stop Believin'" by Journey (1981)
- "Every Breath You Take" by The Police (1983)
- "Girls Just Want to Have Fun" by Cyndi Lauper (1983)
- "Pour Some Sugar on Me" by Def Leppard (1987)
- "Livin' on a Prayer" by Bon Jovi (1986)
- "I Wanna Dance with Somebody" by Whitney Houston (1987)
- "Billie Jean" by Michael Jackson (1983)
- "Rio" by Duran Duran (1982)
- "Everybody Wants To Rule The World" by Tears for Fears (1985)
- "Don't You Forget About Me" by Simple Minds (1985)
- "Video Killed The Radio Star" by The Buggles (1980)

You may have a different thirteen in mind, but I think we can all agree that these thirteen are so choice!

"My radio, believe me, I like it loud, I'm the man with a box that can rock the crowd, Walkin' down the street, to the hardcore beat, While my JVC vibrates the concrete, I'm sorry if you can't understand, But I need a radio inside my hand, Don't mean to offend other citizens, But I kick my volume way past 10, My story is rough, my neighborhood is tough, But I still sport gold, and I'm out to crush, My name is Cool J, I devastate the show, But I couldn't survive without my radio!"

LL Cool J
(Krush Groove - 1985)

Chapter Four
Hip Hop, Grunge, & Fashion

I can't write about music and not mention hip hop and hip hop culture across the 80s and 90s. There was a dramatic change in both music and fashion in that span of twenty years. As we transitioned from the bright and bold styles of the 80s to the grunge and minimalism of the 90s, our musical tastes evolved alongside our wardrobes.

Personally, I prefer the music of the 80s overall, but I was, and still am, a huge fan of 90s Hip Hop and R&B.

Hip Hop's Rise and Fashion Revolution

Hip hop culture had an enormous impact on the fashion world during the 80s and 90s. One of the most iconic fashion moments was when Run DMC famously rocked Adidas tracksuits and sneakers without laces, making them a must-have for virtually any young kid. LL Cool J's Kangol bucket hat became a signature item for him and for the whole genre. I remember everyone wanting a Kangol hat! It was an absolute necessity if you wanted to exude style. I saw so many people try to rock these hats. Some succeeded, many did not!

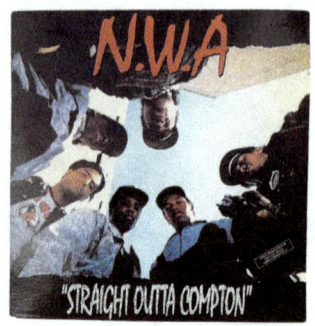

N.W.A STRAIGHT OUTTA COMPTON - First Pressing (Vinyl)

Besides the fashion statements, hip hop music also created some unforgettable moments during that twenty-year span. Public Enemy's *Fight the Power* became an anthem for social change and activism, while N.W.A.'s *Straight Outta Compton* sparked controversy and pushed the boundaries of what was acceptable in music.

The emergence of hip hop also gave rise to breakdancing, a dance style that combined acrobatics, popping, and locking. The cultural movement spread, with breakdancers displaying their skills on sidewalks and in parks across the country.

It's interesting to note that *Breaking* was the only new sport added to the Paris Olympics in June 2024. After a series of controversies, including athlete selection issues and a disappointing (and laughable) performance from Australia's breakdancer, Rachael Gunn (Raygun), Breaking's Olympic future is uncertain.

RAD FACT:

In 1986, Run DMC released **My Adidas**, leading to the first endorsement deal between a hip hop group and a major corporation. This partnership paved the way for future collaborations between musicians and fashion brands, as well as athletes such as **Michael Jordan**.

***

Always Bold 80s

The fashion of the 80s was all about making a statement. We saw the rise of iconic brands like Swatch, Guess Jeans, and Members Only. Michael Jackson's red leather jacket in *Thriller* became an instant classic, and Eddie Murphy's leather jacket in *Beverly Hills Cop* made us all want to be a cool detective like Axel Foley. I remember there were a couple of dudes that somehow got their hands on a Michael Jackson style red leather jacket. It was absolutely hilarious to see, but they still rocked it.

Hair was big and bold, with teased bangs, crimped hair, and lots of hairspray. And I mean lots of hairspray. We wanted to stand out and be noticed, and our fashion choices reflected that.

Fashion and music in the 80s were equally bold. New Wave bands teased different fashion styles, and they influenced young people and adults alike. Remember the fashion style of Duran Duran and The Human League, or A Flock of Seagulls and Culture Club?

RAD FACT:

Madonna's *Like a Virgin* performance at the first MTV Video Music Awards in 1984 caused a sensation (and controversy) with her wedding dress costume and provocative dance moves. At that moment, she became a fashion status symbol and music icon.

***

The Grungy 90s

As the 80s turned into the 90s, we saw a shift in both music and fashion. More subdued and minimalist looks replaced the oversized and bold styles of the 80s. Grunge fashion emerged, inspired by the music of Nirvana, Soundgarden, and Pearl Jam. We saw flannel shirts, ripped jeans, and combat boots become popular. Even high fashion was influenced by grunge, with designers like Marc Jacobs incorporating the look into their collections.

90s Grunge Fashion Ads | JNCO & K-Mart

RAD FACT:

One of the most memorable fashion trends of the 90s was the rise of **JNCO Jeans**. JNCO Jeans were around in the 80s but got popular in the 90s. They made a bold statement with their exaggerated wide-leg designs. Known for their ultra-baggy fit, oversized pockets, and distinctive logo, JNCO Jeans quickly became a symbol of rebellious youth culture.

The music scene in the 90s became more diverse. While grunge dominated the early part of the decade, we also saw the rise of Britpop with bands like Oasis and Blur, the emergence of girl power with the Spice Girls, and the continued evolution of hip hop with artists like Tupac and The Notorious B.I.G.

Grunge music often gets a bad rap, especially with 70s born 80s kids. I'll be the first to admit for some time I absolutely hated it. Over the years, however, I've grown to appreciate it. Have you ever just sat down and listened to *Man In The Box* by Alice in Chains, on vinyl? Or, *Today* by The Smashing Pumpkins? What about *Come As You Are* by Nirvana? There are some incredible and memorable songs that came out of the Grunge scene that are worth exploring. Ever since I started recollecting vinyl records, I've been buying up a few of these grunge gems as I come across them. By the way, if we wave off grunge music, we are also waving off a vast majority of alternative rock from the 90s, and I personally cannot do that. There is just too much wonderful music in that sub-genre.

RAD FACT:

Kurt Cobain's iconic green cardigan, worn during Nirvana's MTV Unplugged performance in 1993, sold at auction for $334,000 in 2019.

***

Choice Trends

Despite the shift towards grunge fashion, some 80s fashion staples remained popular in the 90s. Swatch watches were still a must-have accessory, and Guess Jeans continued to be a favorite among both men and women. Hair trends also shifted, with more natural and effortless styles becoming popular. The 90s saw the rise of the "Rachel" haircut, made famous by Jennifer Aniston's character on *Friends*.

1989 Macy's - Swatch The Cold Hard Facts 'Steeltech' Watch Ad

In music, while new genres emerged, many 80s artists continued to evolve and stay relevant. Madonna reinvented herself with her 1998 album *Ray of Light*, while Michael Jackson and Prince continued to release hit albums throughout the 90s.

Looking back on the fashion and music of the 80s and 90s, it's hard not to laugh at some trends we followed. Who can forget those hilarious baggy parachute pants worn by MC Hammer, or the neon spandex outfits Jane Fonda wore in her workout videos? But despite the questionable fashion choices, we still look back on those trends with fondness.

RAD FACTS

1. Over 20 million Swatch watches sold in 1987 alone.

2. Guess Jeans sales tripled between 1982 and 1984, thanks to their campaigns featuring Claudia Schiffer and Anna Nicole Smith.

3. Michael Jackson's red "Thriller" jacket sold at auction in 2011 for $1.8 million.

4. Ray-Ban Wayfarer sunglasses saw a resurgence in popularity thanks to their appearance in movies like *The Blues Brothers* and *Risky Business*.

5. Aqua Net hairspray reportedly sold over 500 million cans in 1986 at the

height of the big hair trend.

6. Members Only jackets were so popular that the company reportedly sold over 15 million of them in 1984 alone.

7. Nike's Air Jordan line, debuting in 1985, often caused riots at stores upon their release.

8. Reebok Pumps, introduced in 1989, were famously worn by basketball star Dee Brown in the 1991 NBA Slam Dunk Contest

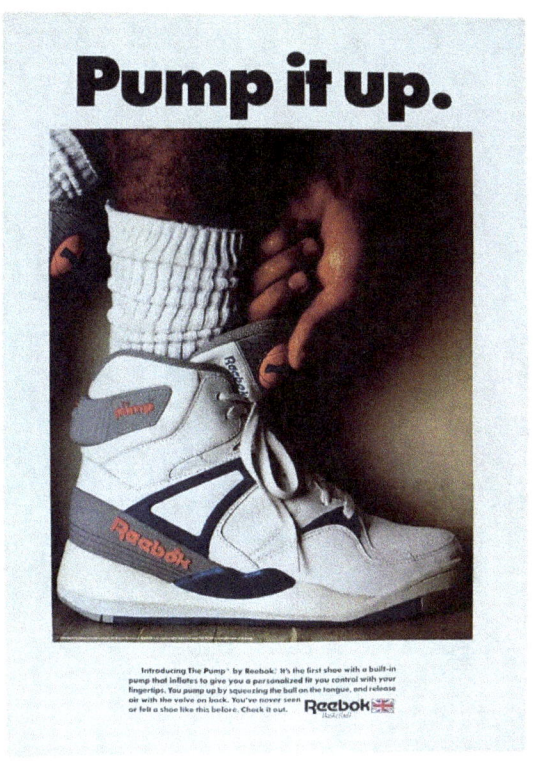

1990 Reebok Pump 'Pump it up.' Advert

"Malfunction. Need Input."

Number 5
(Short Circuit - 1986)

Chapter Five

Dial-Up Daze

A Gen X Love Letter to the Early Internet... When Patience Wasn't Just a Virtue, It Was a System Requirement

SCREEEEEEE... BONG... BEEEEEP... KSSSSHHHHHHH

If you just heard that sound in your head, you are most definitely Gen X. When I've asked younger generations to hear it, they think it's just noise, but Gen X kids have registered the dial-up modem symphony in our minds because it was our living room or bedroom connection to the future at a blazing 56 kilobytes per second (when you were lucky)!

The Hardware Hassle

Remember when a decent computer cost as much as a used car? In the early '90s, a robust IBM-compatible PC with a 486 processor would set you back about $2,000 – that's nearly $4,000 in today's money. Add another $400 for a 14.4k modem, $300 for a chunky monitor, and don't forget the $200 dot-matrix printer that sounded like a tiny jackhammer. For many of us, this represented months of saved paychecks from our first "real" jobs. For me, it was selling candy at a marked up price at school – until I got caught, that is.

But the real ongoing cost was the internet itself. AOL's infamous disk-bombing campaign (first on floppy disks, then on CDs) offered us precious free hours of internet access. After that, you were looking at $20-30 monthly for basic dial-up service – if you stayed within your hour limits. Go over, and you could end up with a bill that would make your dad pull his already thinning hair out!

You've Got Mail

Connecting to the internet was a ceremony that required perfect conditions and sometimes divine intervention. First, you had to ensure nobody was expecting a phone call – because your internet adventure would hijack the phone line. Then came the connection ritual: double-click the AOL icon, listen to the modem's electronic chant, and pray to God that you'd get through on the first try.

You've Got Mail! was a cultural touchstone so significant Lauren Shuler-Donner Productions made a whole movie about it (starring Tom Hanks and Meg Ryan). Email addresses were weird and wonderful things, often hosted on services like CompuServe (remember those numeric ID addresses?) or AOL. Can you think back to your first email address?

RAD FACT:

"You've got mail" was a greeting recorded by Elwood Edwards in 1989 for what would become America Online (AOL)

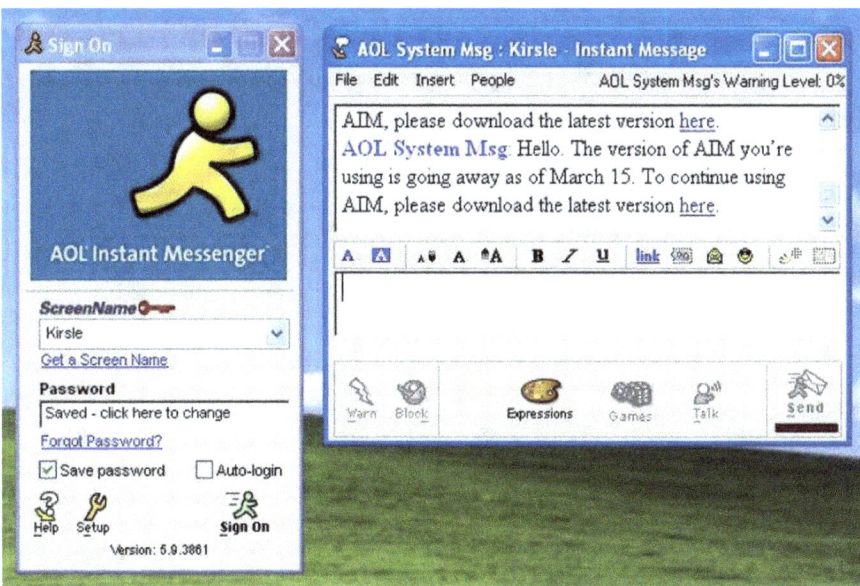

The Wild Wild West... Web

The early web was a lawless frontier where GeoCities pages sparkled with animated GIFs and auto-playing MIDI files. Every website seemed to be "Under Construction" with little animated worker GIFs dutifully chipping away. Comic Sans wasn't ironic – it was the height of sophisticated web design.

Here are a few key milestones that we witnessed:

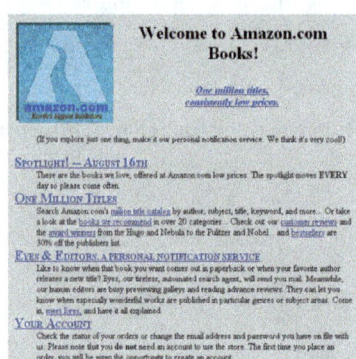

1994: Amazon launches as an online bookstore (books for $20, shipping for $3). The very first book sold on Amazon was *Fluid Concepts and Creative Analogies* by Douglas Hofstadter, a book about artificial intelligence. It was purchased just weeks after the site's launch.

eBay began as *AuctionWeb* in 1995. The first item sold on the platform was a broken laser pointer for $14.83. Surprised, founder Pierre Omidyar contacted the buyer to confirm they knew it was broken. The buyer responded, "I'm a collector of broken laser pointers." This demonstrated the platform's potential for niche markets.

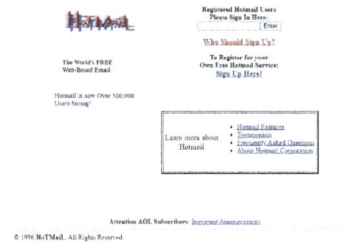

When *Hotmail* launched in July 1996, its founders, Sabeer Bhatia and Jack Smith, chose the name because it included "HTML" (the language used to create web pages). It was originally stylized as *HoTMaiL* to emphasize its web-based nature, which was groundbreaking at the time.

Google began in 1996 as a research project by Larry Page and Sergey Brin, two Stanford University Ph.D. students. By September 1998, Google had officially launched in a garage in Menlo Park, California, setting the stage for its journey to becoming one of the world's most influential tech companies.

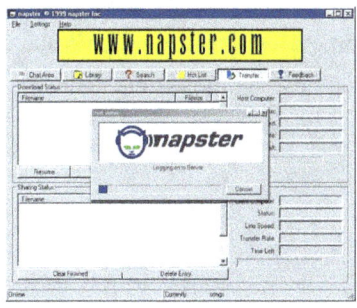

Napster was founded in 1999 by Shawn Fanning and Sean Parker, who were both in their teens. Fanning, just 18 years old at the time, developed Napster as a peer-to-peer (P2P) file-sharing platform to let users share MP3 music files. It became an instant hit among college students and music enthusiasts.

***

The Dot-Com Boom (and Bust)

Remember when Pets.com went from Super Bowl ads to bankruptcy in less than a year?! We saw Amazon's stock price go from $1.50 to $113 back to $5.97, and for those investors that held on, their lives changed! Companies added ".com" to their names and watched their stock prices triple overnight. I even purchased a few .coms by 1999. I still own a few four character domains!

The NASDAQ climbed from 1,000 to 5,000 between 1995 and 2000, making paper millionaires of coffee shop baristas in Silicon Valley. Then came the crash, teaching Gen X yet another lesson about economic reality.

Countless dot-com companies, such as Pets.com, Webvan, and Boo.com, collapsed, wiping out billions of dollars in investor wealth. This was all speculative money. Most of these companies were not tested and lacked financial capital.

Even established tech giants like *Amazon* and *Cisco Systems* experienced significant stock price declines. However, a few companies, such as *Google* and *eBay*, weathered the storm and emerged stronger, demonstrating sustainable business models and long-term growth potential. I was still young in the late 90s and was just starting to make some money, but I understood the dangers of speculation because of the comic book and the sports card market. I was not shocked when some of these companies went under.

***

The Music (Napster) Revolution

Admit it, you were addicted to Napster!

Before *Spotify*, there was *Napster*, and it was glorious (legally questionable, but glorious). Created by Gen Xer Shawn Fanning, *Napster* represented everything we loved about the early internet: it was free, rebellious, and completely transformed an established industry.

Downloading a single song could take 20 minutes or more, and you never knew if you were getting the actual track or a mislabeled file of someone's garage band. Making a digital playlist meant dedicating your phone line for an entire weekend. The RIAA's subsequent crackdown and Metallica's infamous lawsuit marked the end of this brief, beautiful era of musical anarchy.

We can't forget about two other services that made the music revolution a little more bearable: *BearShare* (2000) and *LimeWire* (2000). These services were less impacted and you could expand your music library much faster if you were clever enough to build a few custom systems.

RAD FACTS:

1. The first spam email was sent in 1978, but it didn't become a plague until the mid-90s

2. The dancing baby GIF (aka "Baby Cha-Cha") became the first viral meme in 1996

3. By 1999, it took approximately 30 minutes to download a single MP3 file

4. The original Google servers were housed in LEGO-bright casing

5. The entire internet of 1995 had less data than a single modern HD movie

***

Communities and Chat Rooms

Before social media, we had IRC channels, AOL chat rooms, and bulletin board systems (BBS). These were our digital town squares where you could discuss *X-Files* theories, share *Star Trek* fan fiction, or debate the merits of grunge vs. alternative rock.

The concept of "A/S/L?" (Age/Sex/Location) became a universal internet language, and "cybering" entered the lexicon (though we don't talk about that part).

While the rest of the world was sleeping, we were hunched over beige keyboards, building genuine communities behind ridiculous screen names like Distructodisk1, Grunge-Girl_Seattle, and FrostyRaptor. I used movie character names. We didn't need fancy profile pictures or verified accounts. Our street cred came from how well we could contribute to a conversation about the latest episode of *Friends* or debate whether Mulder and Scully would ever get together.

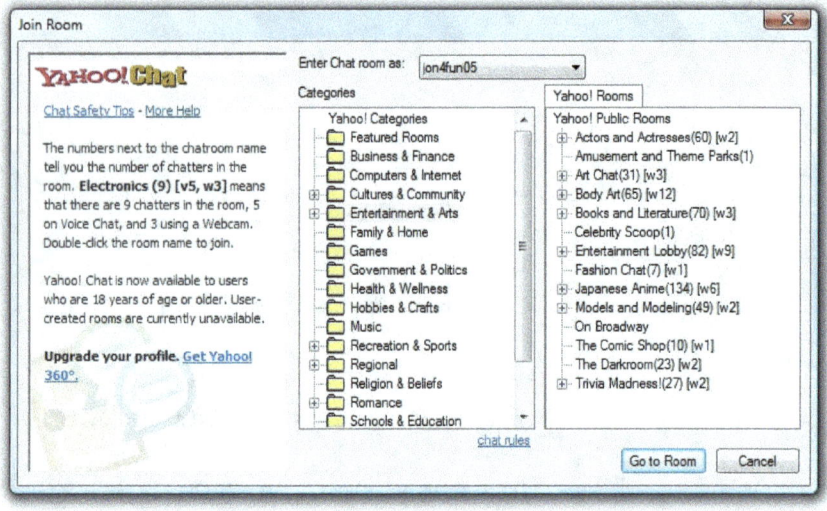

Those IRC channels and BBSs were our testing ground for what would become modern social media, though we did it better. No algorithms, no influencers, no personal brands to maintain—just pure connection based on shared interests and the ability to craft a decent message in ASCII art ¯_(□)_/¯.

We moderated ourselves with nothing but chat room etiquette and the ever-present threat of being booted by a power-tripping SysOp. Looking back, maybe we had it right the first time.

***

Internet Bliss

Looking back, those dial-up days seem almost quaint. Yet, Generation X's experience with the early internet shaped how we approach technology today. We appreciate the convenience of high-speed internet while maintaining a healthy skepticism about technological dependence. I still remember when "going online" was like preparing for an event!

I like the fact that we were there when the internet evolved from a curiosity to a necessity, from a luxury to a utility. We've watched download speeds go from 14.4k to 56k to broadband, each increment feeling like an incredible leap. We survived the Y2K panic (remember stocking up on canned food?), and emerged into the new millennium with optimism.

Today's kids will never know the thrill of successfully downloading a single song overnight, the agony of someone picking up the phone mid-download, or the simple pleasure of finally connecting after the fifth try. But we do, and maybe that's what makes Generation X's relationship with the internet so special – we remember when it was all new, exciting, and full of possibility.

Just don't ask us how many AOL free trial CDs we still have in a box somewhere in the garage!

"Greetings, Starfighter! You have been recruited by the Star League to defend the Frontier against Xur and the Ko-Dan Armada."

Centauri [voice in video game]
(The Last Starfighter - 1984)

Chapter Six

The Arcade Experience

When I explain to younger generations that we used to physically go to a location filled with large machines just to play video games with our friends, they're often dumbfounded. The question they always ask is "Why?" While some of us had home consoles like the Atari or NES (which I'll discuss in the next chapter), the arcade was the social hub for gaming. It was where we met up with friends and inevitably made new ones.

The youth of today might find it hard to believe that gaming wasn't always about live-streaming play throughs on YouTube or shouting into headsets. Before the era of "Live" console gaming, the gaming scene was dominated by dimly lit arcades, often adorned with neon lights, that were a staple in strip malls and movie theater lobbies throughout the 80s and 90s.

If you weren't around during the golden age of arcades, you missed out on a truly unique experience. We spent our allowances there, developing repetitive stress injuries before they even had a name. Playing video games at home just doesn't compare. The satisfying clunk of quarters hitting the machine, the warm glow of the monitors, and that unmistakable arcade scent—a mix of ozone, pizza grease, and the desperate desire to win—it was pure magic.

One of my most cherished memories from my adolescence is the countless afternoons spent at the local 7-Eleven with my best friend. In the late 80s and early 90s, this convenience store had a dedicated arcade game section that was our go-to spot after school. We'd hop on our bikes and head straight there to unwind from a long day of school. The arcade boasted a fantastic lineup of games like *Superman, Mortal Kombat, Street Fighter, Teenage Mutant Ninja Turtles, Golden Axe, Ninja Gaiden, Double Dragon, Ms. Pac-Man, Missile Command,* and the ever-popular but frustratingly often out-of-order *Paperboy.* While the nearby Circle K also had a few arcade games, 7-Eleven's options were superior, and so it was our preferred hangout. It was more than just a place to play games; it was a social hub where we'd catch up with mutual friends, enjoy a Slurpee, indulge in a Snickers bar or see who could chew an entire Big League Chew bubble gum bag in one attempt, and simply enjoy each other's company. Those afternoons at 7-Eleven were a defining part of my transition from childhood to the teenage years, and they remain a source of fond nostalgia to this day.

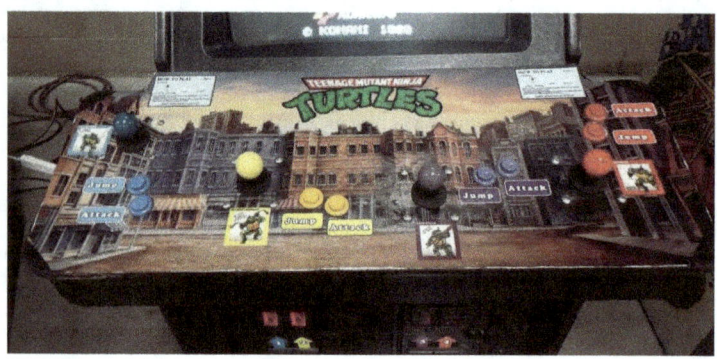

Arcade hierarchy was beautiful in its simplicity. You'd stake your claim at Street Fighter II by placing your quarter on the cabinet's edge – the original "next in line" button. The really hardcore players could make one quarter last for a long time, while the rest of us burned through our paper route money faster than you can say, "HADOUKEN!" And let's not forget about those mythical creatures who could beat *Dragon's Lair* without re-mortgaging their parents' house. The movie *The Wizard* was about this kind of player. I always imagined one day I would get a shot to compete against the top players in the world and win fifty thousand dollars. I'm sure I wasn't the only one.

There are still a few arcades around today. I've also been fortunate enough to meet a few very capable content creators that have built very respectable arcades out of their garage. The arcade spirit is still alive and well, but the golden age couldn't last forever. As home consoles got better and parents grew increasingly convinced that arcades were dens of iniquity (spoiler alert: they kind of were), our beloved institutions faded. It's hard to compete when games were ported with significant improvements on home consoles (i.e. *Bionic Commando*, *Turtles In Time*, *Street Fighter II*, *Mortal Kombat*, *Golden Axe*, and *Streets of Rage*, just to name a few) and could be enjoyed in the comfort of your own home – minus the sticky floors and that one kid who never seemed to leave the Galaga machine.

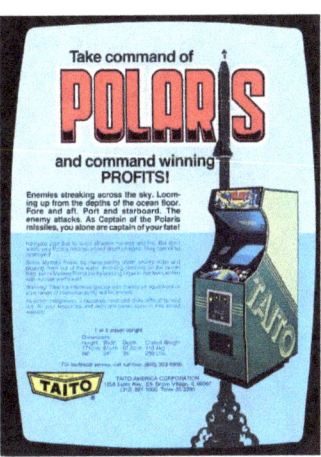

TAITO Polaris Arcade Machine Ad (1980)

Eventually, local arcades spots across America shuttered their doors one by one. The great arcade exodus had begun, and suddenly those "Insert Coin" prompts took on a whole new meaning: game over for an entire culture. Sure, you can still find arcades today – Dave & Buster's tries to capture the magic with their corporate-approved blend of games and alcohol – but it's about as authentic as a Twitter blue checkmark.

Now we're left with our memories and a handful of retro gaming bars where aging Gen Xers can pay $12 for the privilege of playing *Ms. Pac-Man* while sipping craft IPAs. The irony isn't lost on us that we're now dropping the equivalent of 48 quarters per beer to relive our misspent youth. But hey, at least we can tell our kids about the time we lived through the real "player one" era – back when gaming meant actually going out and being social, and the only cloud storage we knew was the collection of tokens in our dresser drawers.

"You have died of dysentery."

Oregon Trail
(First released in 1985 for the Apple II)

Chapter Seven

The Games That Made Us

The home entertainment revolution of the 1980s and 1990s was nothing short of a seismic shift in the way we relaxed and had fun. Video games, once confined to the noisy, coin-operated confines of arcades – which we loved – exploded into our living rooms, bedrooms, and basements. For those of us growing up during those days, we were immersed in these new worlds at our fingertips. Home gaming created new social experiences from within our homes, contributing in part to our shared cultural experience.

Affordable home consoles like the Atari 2600, the Nintendo Entertainment System (NES), and the Sega Genesis democratized gaming. Suddenly, we could immerse ourselves in epic quests, sports simulations, and mind-bending puzzles from the comfort of our own homes. To avoid alerting my dad during late-night gaming sessions, I would pause my game and strategically turn my NES console around. This hid the telltale (beautiful) red glow of the power button, preventing him from discovering my secret *Legend of Zelda* marathon. He had a habit of switching off all electronics, and I was determined to keep my game running.

NINTENDO POWER MAGAZINE clipping | The Legend Of Zelda for NES

While I love the arcade scene, home gaming offered something special unto its own. We could pause, save our progress, and have friends over for multiplayer battles. It created a sense of community and ownership around gaming that had never been seen before. To be clear, the at-home gaming experience of our youth was different from today's live gaming environment. Current games can be highly addictive and toxic, fostering an atmosphere where anonymous interactions often lead to bullying. In contrast, our gaming experiences allowed us to step away and return later without the mental drain and anxiety that can accompany today's multiplayer worlds.

The impact of the at-home gaming revolution extended far beyond the realm of gaming itself. It influenced how we consume media, interact with technology, and even perceive ourselves. It's fascinating how gaming has evolved. There was a time when parents worried that *Dungeons & Dragons* would turn their kids into cult leaders. Now, gaming is everywhere. It's become a part of almost every aspect of our consumer culture, even education. We're living in a gamified world. The home entertainment revolution laid the groundwork for the digital age. It normalized computers and other electronic devices in our homes, paving the way for the internet, smartphones, and the interconnected world we inhabit today. The way we stream movies, listen to music, and even work remotely can all be traced back to those early days of gaming consoles.

1983 Advanced Dungeons and Dragons Video Game Magazine Advertisement | Mattel Electronics, Inc.

For us Gen Xers, the memories of our early gaming experiences are deeply intertwined with our sense of identity and nostalgia. We remember the anticipation (and frustration) of blowing into NES cartridges, the frustration of dying repeatedly in *Contra*, and the joy of finally defeating Bowser in *Super Mario Bros.*

Now let's look at the iconic home gaming consoles we loved playing over the years.

Atari Takes Center Stage

Atari ushered in home gaming. The Atari 2600 was released in the late 1970s. Originally launched in 1977 as the Atari Video Computer System, this unassuming wood-paneled box would become the cornerstone of the home gaming industry. By the early 1980s, the renamed Atari 2600 had found its way into millions of homes, introducing a new form of interactive entertainment to the masses. I was less than a year old when the Atari 2600 was released on September 11, 1977. The Atari 2600 was the first system I really started my gaming journey on in the early 80s.

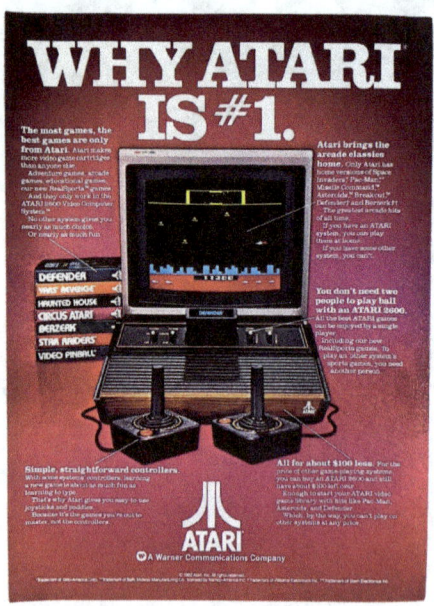

Atari is #1 2600 Print Ad (1982)

The games of this era were simple by today's standards, but they laid the groundwork for everything that would follow. I remember playing *Space Invaders*, *Asteroids*, and *Pac-Man*. My absolute favorites on the Atari 2600 were *Pitfall!* and *Moon Patrol*.

The blocky graphics and simple gameplay mechanics really made these games addictive and fun. To this day, I believe that our generation is so fortunate to have grown up transitioning from console to console, and the Atari was a great springboard for gaming!

However, the Atari era also saw its share of missteps. The infamous *E.T. The Extra-Terrestrial* game, rushed to market in 1982 to coincide with the hit movie, is often cited as one of the worst video games ever made. I absolutely agree. I remember playing that game for the first time and I did not know what was happening. It was extremely frustrating to play. The other game from Atari that was a tremendous disappointment was *Raiders of The Lost Ark*. Is it a coincidence these two games coincided with films? Despite its poor reception, E.T. the game sold over 1.5 million copies, which is a testament to the power of brand recognition and the growing appetite for video games. The failure of E.T. and other hastily produced titles would contribute to the video game crash of 1983, a market correction that threatened to derail the entire industry.

E.T. The Extra-Terrestrial Game Cartridge | Atari 2600
(1982)

As the dust settled from the crash, Atari made another attempt to recapture its former glory with the release of the Atari 7800 in 1986. This new console offered improved graphics and backwards compatibility with 2600 games, but it struggled to gain traction in a market and compete with the Nintendo Entertainment System.

Atari 7800 Ad (1989)

RAD FACT:

At launch, the Atari 7800 was priced at $140, making it significantly cheaper than the Nintendo Entertainment System.

***

Nintendo Redefines the Game

In 1985, Nintendo released the Nintendo Entertainment System (NES) in North America, breathing new life into the home gaming market. We no longer had to break our wrists with the toilet plunger style joystick of the Atari, and we could give our thumb a rest, and allow that indent from the lonely button to fade. Suddenly, we were given the NES controller. It was good to finally have some options! A D-pad? What sorcery is this? And not one, but TWO buttons? It's like going from a unicycle to a Ferrari!

The thing was, the NES wasn't just a new console; it represented a new philosophy in game design and marketing. Nintendo's strict quality control measures and innovative games would set new standards for the industry.

Nintendo Entertainment System (NES) Action Set

Super Mario Bros. became the face of this new era of gaming. The colorful worlds, catchy music, and intuitive gameplay made it accessible to players of all ages. It's-a-me!

Beneath its simple exterior of the NES lay depths that kept players coming back for more. Hidden warp zones, secret power-ups, and the endless pursuit of a higher score turned what could have been a simple platformer into a cultural touchstone.

But Mario was just the beginning. *The Legend of Zelda* introduced players to a vast world of exploration and adventure, with a save feature that allowed for longer, more complex quests. *Metroid* surprised us with its atmospheric sci-fi setting and the revelation that its armored protagonist, Samus Aran, was a woman – a bold statement in the male-dominated world of 1980s video games for sure!

My favorite NES game was *Mike Tyson's Punchout*. I spent hours upon hours playing this game and the fact that I was going to have a shot at boxing against "Iron" Mike was an absolute joy. My dad and I bonded over boxing, so he would occasionally watch me play, and that was everything to me.

Secret Code: Entering 007 373 5963 on the title screen takes you right to fight Mike Tyson, but you better be ready!

The NES era wasn't just about the games themselves, but the culture that grew around them. Nintendo Power magazine became a must-read for young gamers, offering tips, tricks, and tantalizing previews of upcoming titles. Playground conversations revolved around the latest games, with knowledge of secret levels or special moves conferring a certain status among our classmates.

As the 1980s drew to a close, Nintendo solidified its dominance of the home console market. But a new frontier was about to open up, one that would make video games more personal and portable than ever before.

***

Gaming on the Go: The Game Boy Revolution

In 1989, Nintendo once again changed the game with the release of the Game Boy. This handheld console, with its green-tinted screen and chunky design, might not have looked impressive, but it would sell over 118 million units worldwide.

I didn't own a Game Boy until the early 90s, but I sure remember wanting one badly. I was still into playing the NES.

The Game Boy's success was because of its killer game, *Tetris*. This simple yet addictive puzzle game was the perfect showcase for the new portable format. Players could enjoy quick sessions on the bus or longer marathons at home, with the Game Boy's long battery life ensuring the fun didn't stop prematurely.

But *Tetris* was just the beginning. Games like *Super Mario Land* brought Nintendo's flagship franchise to the small screen, while *Pokémon Red and Blue* became a global hit, spawning a multimedia empire that continues to this day.

The Game Boy didn't just change how we played games; it changed where we played them. Suddenly, gaming wasn't confined to the living room. Long car rides, waiting rooms, and even school playgrounds (much to the frustration of teachers) became impromptu gaming arenas. Thanks to the Game Boy, my Etch-A-Sketch and most of my pocket games were retired!

I still have my original Game Boy, but alas, it needs to be repaired. The original Game Boys suffered from power problems, screen problems, and battery issues.

As Nintendo dominated both the home and portable markets, a new challenger was about to emerge, one that would spark the first great console war and push the entire industry in bold new directions.

RAD FACT:

When the Nintendo Game Boy was first released in North America on July 31, 1989, it retailed for $89.99

Nintendo Game Boy DMG-01

***

Sega Does What Nintendon't: The Genesis Era

In 1989, Sega launched the Genesis (known as the Mega Drive outside North America), positioning it as a more powerful, more "mature" alternative to the NES. With its sleek black design and aggressive marketing, Sega aimed to capture the attention of older teen gamers who might have felt they had outgrown Nintendo's family-friendly image.

The Genesis's technical capabilities allowed for more detailed graphics and smoother animation, but it was Sega's mascot that truly set the console apart. *Sonic the Hedgehog*, with his attitude and blazing speed, was the antithesis of the stoic, slow-moving Mario. Sonic's games emphasized momentum and exploration, with sprawling levels that rewarded both quick reflexes and thorough investigation.

But Sonic wasn't the only star in Sega's lineup. *Streets of Rage* brought arcade-style brawling into the living room, while sports games like *NBA Jam* and *Madden NFL* pushed the boundaries of what was possible in digital athletics.

The Genesis era also saw the rise of more mature content in video games, epitomized by the controversy surrounding *Mortal Kombat*. The game's realistic digitized graphics and brutal "fatalities" sparked a national conversation about violence in video games, ultimately leading to the creation of the Entertainment Software Rating Board (ESRB).

This made us want to play violent games even more!

My favorite SEGA Genesis games included *Altered Beast, Castlevania: Bloodlines, Shinobi III: Return of The Ninja Master, Kid Chameleon, Batman, X-Men*, and *John Madden Football '93: Championship Edition*.

RAD FACT:

Altered Beast was the original pack-in game for the Sega Genesis in North America before being replaced by *Sonic the Hedgehog*.

As Sega and Nintendo battled for market supremacy, a new generation of consoles was on the horizon, one that would bring 3D graphics and CD-quality sound into homes around the world.

***

The 16-Bit Wars: Enter The Super Nintendo

In 1991, Nintendo answered Sega's challenge with the Super Nintendo Entertainment System (SNES). This new console brought with it a leap in graphical and audio capabilities, setting the stage for some of the best games of the 1990s.

Super Mario World expanded on everything that made the original Mario games great, introducing new power-ups, secrets, and Yoshi, Mario's dinosaur sidekick. The game's vibrant colors and fluid animation showcased the SNES's capabilities, while its intricate level design kept players coming back long after they'd first rescued Princess Peach.

Super NES Donkey Kong Set

But it was in the role-playing game (RPG) genre that the SNES truly shined. *Final Fantasy III* (known as *Final Fantasy VI* in Japan) brought players an epic storyline with a large cast of memorable characters, complemented by Nobuo Uematsu's stirring musical score. *Chrono Trigger*, with its time-traveling plot and multiple endings, pushed the boundaries of what was possible in video game storytelling.

The SNES era also saw the rise of the fighting game genre. *Street Fighter II* became a phenomenon, its colorful cast of world warriors and intricate combo system inspiring friendly (and not-so-friendly) competition in living rooms and arcades alike.

I loved playing *The Adventures of Batman & Robin, Super Double Dragon, Teenage Mutant Ninja Turtles: Turtles in Time, Mega Man X, Super Mario Kart*, and *Super Metroid* on the SNES!

As the 16-bit era progressed, both Sega and Nintendo continued to innovate. Sega's CD add-on for the Genesis allowed for full-motion video and CD-quality audio, while Nintendo experimented with the Super FX chip, which allowed for rudimentary 3D graphics in games like *Star Fox*.

***

The Nintendo 64: A New Dimension in Gaming

In 1996, Nintendo once again revolutionized the industry with the release of the Nintendo 64. What a console!

This powerful system brought true 3D gaming into the home, along with an innovative controller design that included an analog stick for precise movement in 3D environments. I've got to admit, it is my least favorite joystick of any system. The stick itself never lasted. I think I own a dozen of them, and that's after having discarded a dozen over the last twenty years because the joystick broke off!

The games were great though!

N64 Launch Edition

Super Mario 64 served as the system's flagship title, reimagining the Mario franchise in three dimensions. Players were no longer constrained to moving left and right; now they could explore vast, open environments, collecting stars and uncovering secrets. The game's camera system, while sometimes frustrating, set the standard for how 3D games would be played for years to come.

The Legend of Zelda: Ocarina of Time took the sense of adventure from previous Zelda games and expanded it into a sweeping epic. Its time-travel mechanic, allowing players to switch between young and adult Link, added depth and enhanced both the gameplay and storytelling. The game's impact was so significant that it's still frequently cited as one of the greatest video games ever made.

The N64 also excelled in multiplayer gaming. *GoldenEye 007*, one of my favorite games, and one that I still play today, brought first-person shooter action to consoles in a way that had never been seen before. Its four-player split-screen mode became a staple of dorm rooms and basement hangouts. *Mario Kart 64* took the karting formula established on the SNES and added vertigo-inducing 3D tracks and new battle modes that kept us entertained for hours upon hours.

As impressive as the N64 was, it faced stiff competition from a newcomer to the video game market – one that would change the industry forever.

***

The PlayStation Era

In 1994, Sony launched the PlayStation, marking its entry into the video game console market. The PlayStation's use of CD-ROM technology allowed for larger games with full-motion video cut scenes and CD-quality audio, pushing video game storytelling and presentation to new heights.

Sony Playstation (PS1) System & Games Target Promo (1999)

Final Fantasy VII became the PlayStation's flagship title, its pre-rendered backgrounds and cinematic cut-scenes bringing a new level of visual spectacle to console RPGs. I still have my original copy! The game's story, dealing with themes of environmentalism and corporate power, resonated with so many of us and showcased the potential for video games to tackle complex, mature themes.

Then there was *Metal Gear Solid*. Released in 1998, the game pushed the boundaries of both gameplay and storytelling. Its emphasis on stealth over direct confrontation was innovative for the time, and its fourth-wall-breaking moments – like Psycho Mantis "reading" the player's memory card – remain iconic to this day.

Metal Gear Solid | Sony PlayStation 1 (PS1)

The PlayStation era also saw the rise of survival horror as a major genre. Do you remember playing *Resident Evil* for the first time?! The game's blend of puzzle-solving, resource management, and jump scares kept us on the edge of our seats, while Silent Hill's psychological horror and disturbing imagery pushed the boundaries of what was acceptable in mainstream gaming. I tried playing *Silent Hill* in a pitch black room early on, and let me tell you, it was pure nightmare fuel!

Sony knew it needed to cater to our younger selves as well. *Crash Bandicoot* became Sony's de facto mascot, his wacky antics and challenging platforming providing a more lighthearted alternative to some of the system's darker fare. *Spyro the Dragon* offered colorful worlds to explore, while *PaRappa the Rapper* introduced the rhythm game genre to a wider audience.

The first PlayStation was really something special. My favorite PlayStation games included *Final Fantasy VII*, Tony *Hawk's Pro Skater 3*, *Rayman*, *Resident Evil*, *Metal Gear Solid*, *Tomb Raider*, and *Medal of Honor*.

Tomb Raider | Sony PlayStation (PS1)

RAD FACT:

The PlayStation was originally intended to be a collaboration between Sony and Nintendo. Sony was developing a CD-ROM add-on for the Super Nintendo, but Nintendo suddenly backed out of the deal. This led Sony to develop the PlayStation as its own standalone console.

***

The Dreamcast: Sega's Swan Song

In 1999, Sega made one last push for console dominance with the Dreamcast. This incredibly innovative system was the first to include a built-in modem for online play, which was groundbreaking, and foreshadowed the connected gaming experiences that would become standard in later console generations.

Games like *Sonic Adventure* brought Sega's mascot into the 3D realm, while *Shenmue* pushed the boundaries of open-world game design. *Jet Set Radio's* cel-shaded graphics and awesome soundtrack captured the sound of urban youth culture, and *Crazy Taxi's* frantic gameplay made it an instant classic.

Unfortunately, despite its innovations, the Dreamcast struggled to compete with Sony's PlayStation 2, which launched in 2000. Sega would eventually exit the hardware market, marking the end of their contribution in console gaming.

Sega Dreamcast

I was really disappointed when the Dreamcast faded. It's a wonderful system that I believe really deserved to be around much longer. The console has been making a comeback in the reseller market though, and that's been wonderful to see.

***

The PlayStation 2: Gaming Enters a New Millennium

The PlayStation 2, launched in 2000, would become the best-selling video game console of all time. Its ability to play DVDs made it an attractive option for families looking for an all-in-one entertainment device, while its vast library of games catered to every taste and interest.

Sony Playstation 2 (PS2) System "Sears" & "Target" Print Ads

The new iterations of *Grand Theft Auto* (GTA) revolutionized open-world game design. The sprawling cityscape and non-linear gameplay offered us so much freedom to explore. *Kingdom Hearts* blended Square's RPG expertise with Disney's beloved characters, creating a unique crossover that appealed to fans of both companies.

The PlayStation 2 for me was very much like opening the box to the original Nintendo Entertainment System. I just knew the PS2 was going to change things.

Do you remember how fun it was to play *Gran Turismo*? Or how about *Ratchet & Clank*? I loved *Need For Speed*, and I spent hours upon hours playing *SOCOM: US Navy Seals*. And who could forget *Star Wares: Battle Front*?!

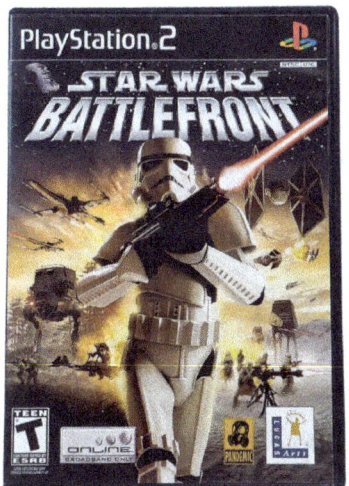 

Star Wars Battlefront | Sony PlayStation 2 (PS2)

As we entered the new millennium, video games had evolved from simple diversions to complex, narrative-driven experiences. The games we played as children had grown up with us, tackling mature themes and pushing the boundaries of interactive storytelling.

Having grown up Gen X, video games were more than just a pastime – they were a fundamental part of our life. In so many ways, we witnessed and took part in the evolution of a new art form.

Early gaming shaped our imaginations, honed our problem-solving skills, and brought us together in ways that previous generations could scarcely have imagined. They taught us the value of perseverance (how many times did we fight that seemingly unbeatable boss?), the joy of exploration, and the importance of teamwork. I will always cherish playing *Double Dragon* with my friends in Oak Park, Michigan!

As we've grown older, many of us have maintained our love for gaming, sharing our favorite classics with our own children or rediscovering them through remasters and online emulators. The gaming industry we helped build as enthusiastic consumers has become a global juggernaut, surpassing both film and music in terms of revenue.

Yet for all the advancements in graphics and storytelling, there's still something magical about those early games. Perhaps it's nostalgia, or perhaps it's a recognition of the creativity required to build entire worlds out of a handful of pixels and a limited color palette.

Whatever the case, those pixelated games of our youth defined our generation. Today, retro gaming is a shared language for Gen X kids, a specifically unique experience that continues to bind us together.

Metroid | Nintendo Entertainment System (NES)

Billy: So you got a job, where you play with all these toys?

Josh: Yup!

Billy: And they're gonna pay you for that?!

Josh: Yup!

Billy: SUCKERS!!

(BIG - 1988)

Chapter Eight
The Toys We Grew Up With

The toys we grew up with were indeed special. They still are. Auction sites offer a huge marketplace for vintage toys, and resellers are constantly hunting for toys from the 80s and 90s because they know we will pay a pretty penny to recollect what we grew up with.

I love that, but I also hate it too. Do you know how hard it is to get a good deal on a Castle Grayskull today? Forget about it!

The toys we played with not only shaped our youth, they also inspired us and made us more creative. It's unreal how they continue to impact culture and entertainment today. 80s and 90s toys have stood the test of time for sure.

It wasn't just action figures or dolls, or plush toys that ruled. We had incredible board games too!

Board games like Hungry Hungry Hippos and Battleship, Hotels, Solar Quest, Mouse Trap, Trouble, Axis & Allies, Risk, Shark Attack, Clue, Connect Four, Life, Dweebs, Geeks & Weirdos (yes, that was a game from the 80s), Double Trouble, and electronic games like Simon, as well! There are just too many to name.

We had some of the wackiest toys as well. Do you remember Mad Balls, or Popples, Boglins, My Pet Monster, or Garbage Pail Kids? These fringe toys definitely reflected the creativity from the great decades.

We also benefited from the brilliant tech advances that toys inspired. Toys like Transformers, Voltron, Tamagotchis, and electronic toys like Teddy Ruxpin, and Tiger Electronics handheld games offered a mix of new ideas, interaction, and storytelling that was new back then.

A lot of these toys got a tremendous boost from TV shows, movies, and comics, which made them even more important historically as well within our shared experience. Some of my most successful and engaging posts on my Instagram page come from toys I post about. People still feel nostalgic about these toys because of how much they meant to us who grew up in that time.

I was in my teens in the 1990s and I was getting interested in other things rather than toys, but I truly admired toy design through the 90s. I remember when Batman: The Animated Series toys dropped and I couldn't help myself, and I bought several of the figures. I was in my early twenties when I bought every single action figure from the *Star Wars Phantom Menace* line. What an incredible investment that has been. I'm joking, obviously.

***

The 1980s: When Toys Came to Life

Let's embark on a brief journey that covers some of the most important toy lines of the 1980s. There is no way we could cover every toy line, so I'm focusing on the toys I either played with myself, or that my family members played with.

The 1980s ushered in a new age of toy innovation, blending innovative technology with imaginative storytelling. We saw the birth of toy lines that would become iconic, often backed by cartoons that blurred the line between entertainment and advertisement. Did we care if the cartoons were half hour long advertisements? Not at all. In fact, we absolutely loved the cartoons, and they were a wonderful way to imagine the scenarios when we played with our friends.

Some of my fondest memories are of digging small trenches in my front yard with my neighborhood friends and playing out the adventures with our action figures.

Transformers: More Than Meets the Eye

In 1984, Hasbro unleashed the Transformers upon an unsuspecting world. These robots in disguise had the unique ability to change from vehicles and everyday objects into heroic Autobots or villainous Decepticons. The accompanying animated series and comic books expanded the Transformers universe, creating a rich mythology.

Remember *Transformers: The Movie*? One of the saddest moments of my childhood was watching Optimus Prime die after being wounded in battle by Megatron. Two things happened the day I saw that animated film;

1. I cried while watching a cartoon.

2. I despised Hot Rod for interfering in the battle that opened up the opportunity to grab the surprisingly small blaster and end Optimus with it!

I still can't watch the scene without getting emotional about it (and angrier at Hot Rod).

Transformers had an immediate and lasting impact on culture. The sound of plastic clashing, the roar of imaginary engines, the thrill of transforming our Transformers from robots to vehicles, it was more than just playing with toys. "Autobots, roll out!" was the battle cry for every kid playing with the toys. Today, the franchise continues to thrive with blockbuster movies, new toy lines, and a fanbase that spans generations.

***

He-Man and the Masters of the Universe: The Power of Grayskull

Mattel's He-Man and the Masters of the Universe line debuted in 1982, bringing the sword and sorcery genre to the toy aisle. The muscular hero and his colorful cast of allies and enemies were a hit, spawning an animated series that took over after-school television. I remember running home as fast as I could so I wouldn't miss an episode.

This might be hard to believe, but one day, there was talk of a fight between two classmates scheduled to take place after school. This was a common thing in Detroit, so don't be shocked. Well, just prior to school getting out, we heard the classmates had declared a truce because they found common ground. That common ground was they both watched *He-Man and the Masters of The Universe* after school and if they were to fight, they would likely miss the episode. If I really think back, I believe we experienced fewer after school fights thanks to Eternia! So let there be no one to question the power of 80s cartoons!

He-Man's impact extended beyond sales figures. The toy line and its accompanying media included action figures for girls. She-Ra was a massive hit. Many young girls joined in the battles to save Eternia from Skeletor and Hordak. Something we all loved about the cartoon series is that it also tackled moral lessons, often ending episodes with insights that helped us understand certain situations as kids, such as stranger danger, believing in ourselves even if we fail at something the first time, and even beach safety!

***

Teenage Mutant Ninja Turtles: Heroes in a Half-Shell

Emerging from the pages of an indie comic book, the Teenage Mutant Ninja Turtles exploded onto the scene when Playmates Toys released the action figure line in 1988. Leonardo, Donatello, Raphael, and Michelangelo, along with their rat sensei Splinter and a host of mutated villains, brought the sewers of New York City to life in our playrooms. We were also introduced to one of the greatest villains of all time, the Shredder!

The Turtles' success was a testament to the power of cross-media promotion. The animated series, which debuted in 1987, catapulted the franchise to new heights. I consider the cartoon intro one of the top five greatest cartoon intros of all time!

We were saying catchphrases like "Cowabunga!" and "Bodacious!" I drop "Totally Tubular" at least once a month. We loved the characters because they were everything we wanted to be, which were awesome, strong, ninja skilled, and pizza eating heroes.

The franchise has shown remarkable staying power, with multiple reinventions over the decades keeping the Turtles relevant for new generations.

I would even venture to say that Teenage Mutant Ninja Turtles is the greatest media franchise of all time.

***

My Little Pony: Friendship is Magic (and Marketable)

I never played with My Little Pony, but my sisters did. Therefore, I would be remiss if I didn't mention this iconic toy brand. They loved the toy line. Hasbro's My Little Pony galloped onto the scene in 1982, offering a softer alternative to the action-oriented toys that were dominating the market. Yes, yes, there was Barbie, but My Little Pony was fresh and full of lore. These colorful equines, with their brushable manes and tails, became a staple of many childhoods, especially among young girls.

A few years ago, I heard an interesting term for dudes who love My Little Pony and collect the toys— Bronies! For a little while, there was even an annual convention called BronyCon. I'm not kidding.

So yeah, My Little Pony was huge, and still sort of is.

The toy line's success demonstrated the market's appetite for gentler, more nurturing play experiences. My Little Pony encouraged imaginative storytelling and social play, aspects that would become increasingly important in toy design. The brand's enduring popularity has led to multiple revivals, including a recent iteration that attracted the unexpectedly diverse fanbase.

RAD FACT:

My Little Pony was created by toy designer Bonnie Zacherle, who initially pitched the idea of a pony toy to Hasbro in the early 1980s. Inspired by her love for horses, Zacherle wanted to create a toy that captured the magical appeal of ponies for young children. The original concept was called "My Pretty Pony," but it was later rebranded and downsized to the now-iconic My Little Pony in 1983.

***

G.I. Joe: A Real American Hero

G.I. Joe underwent a significant transformation in the 1980s, shrinking from 12-inch action figures to a 3.75-inch scale. This change allowed Hasbro to create a plethora of characters and vehicles, each with distinct personalities and specialties. Before the 3.75-inch scale action toys, the larger articulated figures with detailed clothing were the big thing. I never played with those figures. The relaunch in 1982 under the subtitle "A Real American Hero" revitalized the brand for a new generation. My generation.

G.I. Joe's influence extended beyond playtime. The animated series and comic books tackled complex themes of loyalty, duty, and global conflict, albeit in a simplified manner suitable for young audiences. The franchise's diverse cast of characters provided a range of role models and sparked discussions about representation in media.

Some of my favorite G.I. Joe figures included Snake Eyes, Storm Shadow, Shipwreck, Spirit, Sgt. Slaughter, Beach Head, Cobra Vipers, Serpentor, and the original Cobra Commander. Tomax and Xamot were some of the first G.I. Joes I earned as a reward for doing my chores above and beyond. My dad bought them for me at K-Mart in the early 80s!

***

The Toy Line I Wanted The Most From The 80s

One of the more underappreciated toy lines was ThunderCats. The *ThunderCats* toy line was released by LJN in late 1985, shortly after the cartoon series debuted in January of that year.

ThunderCats follows a group of cat-like humanoid aliens from the planet Thundera. After their home world is destroyed, the ThunderCats, led by their young leader Lion-O, flee to the planet Third Earth. There, they battle the evil sorcerer Mumm-Ra and various other villains who seek to destroy them and seize the powerful Sword of Omens, which grants Lion-O the ability to see far-off events and call upon the ThunderCats for aid. The cartoon is known for its fantasy-steeped storytelling, unique characters, and the iconic battle cry, "ThunderCats, ho!"

I deeply connected with the story of the ThunderCats, as my family, too, was forced to flee our home, living under the constant fear of persecution. Having secured asylum in the United States, we loved our new home and new life tremendously. The ThunderCats were a family, and I am the oldest of five, so I also related to their struggle and the way they stuck together as one unit.

Each figure was designed with attention to the unique characteristics of the show's iconic characters, such as Lion-O's Sword of Omens and light-up eyes or Mumm-Ra's transformation feature. The toys stood out for their impressive articulation and accessories, allowing kids to recreate epic battles from the show.

What made the ThunderCats toy line especially cool was it blended fantasy and science fiction elements, embodied in both the characters and the vehicles, like the Thundertank. I still own an original Thundertank, complete in the box!

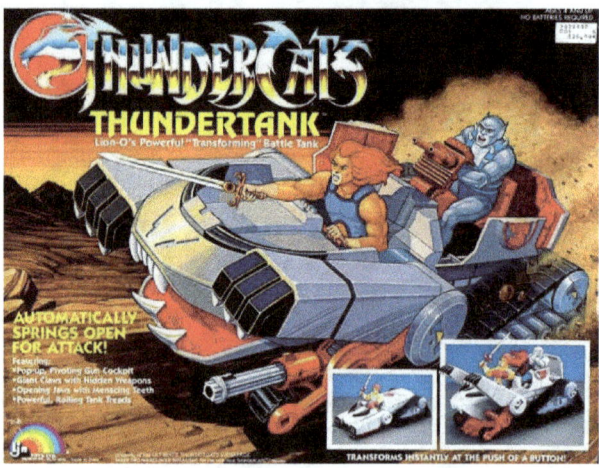

The line also included imaginative play sets, such as the Cat's Lair (basically the Castle Grayskull for the Thundercats), which served as the ThunderCats' headquarters.

The figures were gigantic compared to most other toys, and each figure was designed with attention to the unique characteristics of the show's characters, such as

Lion-O's Sword of Omens and his light-up eyes or Mumm-Ra's transformation feature. Mumm-Ra had two figures, each representing the different form of Mumm-Ra:

Mumm-Ra (The Mummy Form): This figure depicted Mumm-Ra in his original, decrepit mummy form, as seen in the cartoon when he's in his weakened state. The figure was designed to capture his ancient, sinister look, with tattered bandages wrapping his body and a hooded cloak. Despite his frail appearance, this version of Mumm-Ra was central to the show's plot, often seen in his sarcophagus plotting against the ThunderCats.

Mumm-Ra (The Ever-Living): The second figure represented Mumm-Ra in his powerful, transformed state, known as Mumm-Ra the Ever-Living. This version was larger and more muscular, showcasing Mumm-Ra after he has called upon the "Ancient Spirits of Evil" to transform him into a mighty and terrifying warrior. The figure featured dark red eyes that would light up when the Power Ring was used, a trademark headpiece with two snakes, a battle-matic action lever to move the arms, and a large and small dagger. This form of Mumm-Ra was more imposing, allowing kids to recreate the intense battles between Mumm-Ra and the ThunderCats.

I just loved everything about this toy line, and I still do. It's one of the few toy lines I still collect.

***

OTHER NOTABLE 1980S TOY LINES

Below I'm listing the more notable and important toy lines from the 1980s. I intend to include toy lines from the 1990s in future Editions. There are enough toy lines introduced in the 1980s to fill a book on their own.

- Cabbage Patch Kids: These adoptable dolls created a frenzy, teaching lessons about nurturing and individual uniqueness.

- Rubik's Cube: This puzzle sensation challenged minds and spawned countless imitators.

- Nintendo Entertainment System: While not strictly a toy, this gaming console revolutionized home entertainment. I devote time to it in the gaming chapter of this book.

- Care Bears: These cuddly bears with their tummy symbols promoted emotional intelligence through play.

- Pound Puppies: Combining the popular trends of adoption and animal care, these plush dogs found homes in millions of bedrooms.

TENDERHEART Care Bear (1983)

***

TOP 10 BEST-SELLING TOYS OF THE 1980S

1. Pound Puppies - 30-35 million units sold: Created by Mike Bowling and sold by Tonka

2. Strawberry Shortcake - 25-32 million units sold: Designed by Muriel Fahrion for American Greetings

3. Care Bears - 40 million units sold: Created by artist Elena Kucharik and licensed to be sold by Kenner Toys

4. Cabbage Patch Kids - 65 million units sold: Created by Xavier Roberts in 1978. Coleco licensed the rights to sell the toys

5. He-Man and the Masters of the Universe - 70 million units sold: Created by Roger Sweet and developed by Mattel in 1981

6. Teenage Mutant Ninja Turtles - 100 million units sold, becoming one of the most successful toy franchises of the late 80s and early 90s. Created by Kevin Eastman and Peter Laird as comic book characters, the toy line was produced and developed Playmates Toys

7. My Little Pony - 150 million units sold: Created by Bonnie Zacherle, a designer at Hasbro, in 1981. Hasbro launched the toy line in 1983

8. Transformers - 300 million units sold: The toy line originated as a collaboration between Japanese toy companies Takara and Hasbro.

9. Rubik's Cube - 350 million units sold: Invented by Erno Rubik, a Hungarian architect and professor, in 1974. It was initially called the "Magic Cube." The toy was licensed by Ideal Toy Corp in 1980

10. G.I. Joe - 375 million units sold: Larry Hama, a writer for Marvel, played a key role in shaping the G.I. Joe mythos that we all grew up on the 80s. The G.I. Joe toys from this "Real American Hero" line were licensed and distributed by Hasbro.

RAD FACT:

The Transformers toy line was created by merging two separate Japanese toy lines: Diaclone and Microman. Hasbro bought the rights to both, rebranded them, and created the Transformers universe we know today.

***

The 1990s: Digital Dreams and Pocket Monsters

As our generation entered our teens and early adulthood in the late 80s and 90s, the toy industry evolved to meet changing tastes and technological advancements. The 1990s saw the rise of electronic toys and games, as well as franchises that would define the decade and beyond. Below I list some of the most important electronic toy innovations of the 1990s.

***

Pokémon: Gotta Catch 'Em All

Pokémon burst onto the scene in 1996 in Japan, reaching Western shores in 1998. What began as a pair of Game Boy games quickly expanded into a multimedia empire encompassing trading cards, animated series, movies, and countless toys and merchandise.

The impact of Pokémon on popular culture cannot be overstated. It introduced a new form of collectible gameplay that combined strategy, luck, and social interaction. The franchise's ethos of friendship, perseverance, and the bond between humans and creatures resonated with children worldwide. Pokémon's success paved the way for other monster-collecting franchises and demonstrated the power of transmedia storytelling.

***

Tamagotchi: Digital Pets in Your Pocket

Bandai's Tamagotchi, launched in 1996, brought the responsibilities of pet ownership into the digital age. These egg-shaped keychain devices housed virtual pets that required feeding, cleaning, and attention. The Tamagotchi craze swept across playgrounds, with children (and even adults) obsessively caring for their digital dependents.

Tamagotchi's popularity highlighted the growing integration of technology into play. It also sparked discussions about responsible pet ownership and time management, as children juggled their real-world responsibilities with the demands of their virtual pets.

***

Mighty Morphin Power Rangers: Teenagers with Attitude

Adapted from the Japanese Super Sentai series, *Mighty Morphin Power Rangers* exploded onto American television in 1993. The accompanying toy line from Bandai capitalized on the show's popularity, offering action figures, costumes, and roleplay items that allowed children to become their favorite Rangers. The Power Rangers toy line was one of the first to introduce more complex sound effects in their electronic toys. The Power Morpher had really cool light and sound effects. So did the Dragon Dagger from the Green Ranger and the Saba Sword from the White Ranger.

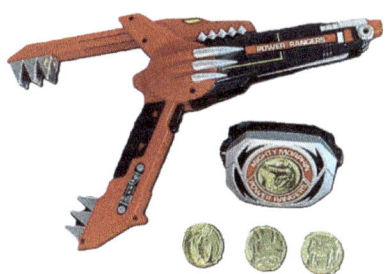

Power Rangers' impact extended beyond toy sales. The diverse cast provided representation for children of various backgrounds, and the show's themes of teamwork and personal growth resonated with its young audience. The franchise's longevity, with numerous iterations over the decades, speaks to its enduring appeal.

***

Beanie Babies: The Collectible Craze

Ty Inc.'s Beanie Babies, introduced in 1993, became more than just stuffed animals—they were a cultural phenomenon. These small, bean-filled plush toys, each with its own name and "birthday," sparked a collecting frenzy that extended well beyond children to adult collectors.

The Beanie Babies craze offered lessons in supply and demand, with limited editions and "retirements" driving up perceived value. Although the Beanie Babies bubble eventually burst, we cannot underestimate their impact on collecting culture and the toy industry's approach to artificial scarcity.

***

Furby: The AI Pet Before Its Time

Tiger Electronics' Furby, launched in 1998, was a technological marvel for its time. This electronic pet could "learn" English, starting with its own *Furbish* language and gradually incorporating more English phrases. Furby pet toys were equal parts fascinating and unnerving, with their ability to "wake up" and speak seemingly unprompted.

Furby's success pointed to the growing interest in interactive, "intelligent" toys. It paved the way for more advanced AI-driven toys and sparked discussions about the role of technology in children's play and development.

OTHER NOTABLE 1990S TOY LINES

- Pogs: This simple game of cardboard discs became a playground sensation and collector's item.

- Polly Pocket: These miniature dolls in compact cases offered portable play for a new generation.

- Nerf: While introduced earlier, Nerf expanded significantly in the '90s with new blasters and sports equipment.

- Magic: The Gathering: This trading card game revolutionized tabletop gaming and spawned countless imitators.

- Sky Dancers: These flying dolls combined action and fantasy play, despite safety concerns.

TOP 10 BEST-SELLING TOYS OF THE 1990S

1. Pokémon Trading Cards - 30 billion cards sold, $10.5 billion revenue
2. Beanie Babies - 500 million units sold, $6 billion revenue
3. Furby - 40 million units sold, $1.8 billion revenue
4. Tamagotchi - 82 million units sold, $1.7 billion revenue
5. Power Rangers Action Figures - 250 million units sold, $1.5 billion revenue
6. Pogs - 350 million units sold, $1.2 billion revenue
7. Barbie (1990s editions) - 700 million units sold, $1.1 billion revenue
8. Nerf (1990s product lines) - 100 million units sold, $1 billion revenue
9. Super Soaker - 200 million units sold, $900 million revenue
10. Polly Pocket - 150 million units sold, $800 million revenue

***

80s and 90s Toys Rocked!

The toys of the 80s and 90s left an unforgettable imprint on Generation X, truly shaping our childhood. As we've grown up, there's no doubt we have carried our love for these toys into adulthood. When I walk into my studio and look at the shelves full of toys from the time I grew up, I'm filled with so much joy.

As kids, we didn't have the various (and very distracting) electronics available to kids today, so toys were a large part of our personal activity time, as well as the way we bonded with our friends and family. We created our own unique play experiences with the toys we had.

When *Teenage Mutant Ninja Turtles: Mutant Mayhem* was released in theaters in 2023, I went out and bought the entire toy line for my kids. Not only did they love the toys, but I also noticed that they played with them a lot more than most of their other toys. The TMNT toy line has produced a fairly consistent product line, so these toys were like the ones I played with when I was a kid. Even though I get my sons toys from newer toy lines, they tend to lose interest in them pretty fast. What I found fascinating was the TMNT toys' consistent formula of over-the-top, colorful, and large-scale characters still resonated with my sons. I think that's because they discovered this approach worked back in my day, and frankly, it hasn't changed.

I sometimes stumble on really cool toys when I'm out and about, and I admire the articulation and work that has gone into them. It will be interesting to see if toys will remain part of the childhood experience in the next two or three generations or if childhood entertainment becomes purely digital. I know for me and my generation, I can't imagine life back in my day without G.I. Joes, Transformers, Masters of The Universe, or ThunderCats!

The Real Ghostbusters Fire Station Headquarters Playset | Kenner (1984)

To PLAY is human.
To REWIND is divine!

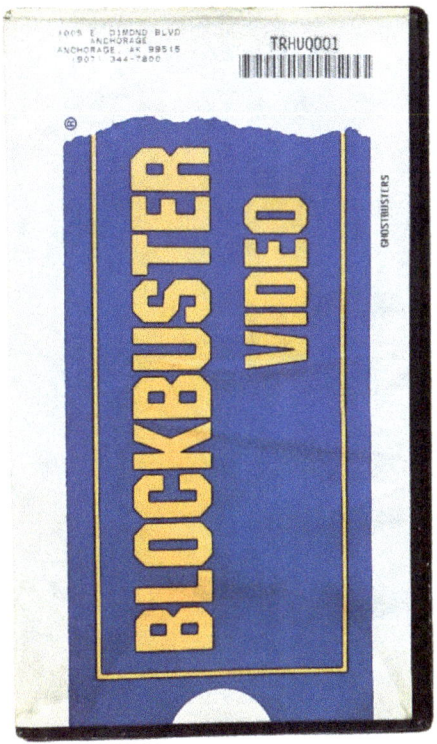

Blockbuster Video
(Wow! What a Difference!)

Chapter Nine
Enter The VHS

Every Gen X kid remembers the format war between two competing videotape technologies: VHS and Betamax (Beta). Both formats were introduced in the mid-1970s, but it wasn't until the 1980s that the rivalry between them really heated up.

Betamax was introduced by Sony in 1975 and offered superior picture and sound quality compared to VHS. However, it was more expensive and could only record up to one hour of video on a single tape. JVC introduced VHS in 1976 and was cheaper, more widely available, and could record up to two hours of video on a single tape.

Sony Betamax and Panasonic VHS ads | 1980s

As a kid, I remember Betamax was more popular among early adopters and enthusiasts who valued its superior picture and sound quality. I remember seeing ads about Betamax in newspapers thrown out in the streets. Sometimes I'd pick up the papers to glance at them because, I'm ashamed to say, I thought maybe it was smut, which was commonly discarded in the streets in Detroit. But VHS gained ground by offering longer recording times and more affordable machines. As the popularity of VHS grew, more movies and TV shows were released on the format, creating an extensive library of content that could be rented or purchased at video stores.

When we moved to Oak Park, MI in the late 80s, I had a neighbor whose dad was an early adopter. He owned both Betamax and VHS players and tapes. He also had a vast library of adult films that I stumbled on, but that story is for another time.

The format war was not just about technology, but also about licensing and marketing. VHS was marketed as the more consumer-friendly format, with more companies producing VHS players and tapes. Meanwhile, Sony maintained tight control over Betamax, limiting the number of manufacturers who could produce machines and tapes.

In the end, VHS emerged as the clear winner of the format war, largely because of its wider availability, longer recording times, and lower costs. By the mid-80s, VHS had become the dominant format for home video, and the Betamax format was largely phased out.

Personally, I love the Betamax format. I thought the work Sony put into the cover art was incredible, and I'm still a fan of the format today. I love the look of the Beta cassettes compared to VHS.

Here are some key points that stand out to me about the VHS/BETA saga of the 80s:

- Despite being the dominant format for home video in the 1980s, many in the film industry initially dismissed VHS as a low-quality, inferior format. Some directors and producers even refused to release their films on VHS, preferring instead to stick with theatrical releases or wait for the Betamax format to catch on.

- One of the most famous movies to be released only on Betamax was *The Star Wars Holiday Special* in 1978. The TV special aired once on CBS and was never rebroadcast, but a home video release was planned. Because Betamax was perceived as the higher-quality format, the special was only released on Betamax and not VHS.

- Despite being phased out in the 80s, Betamax has remained popular among videophiles and enthusiasts, even to this day! Some indie filmmakers even continue to use Betamax cameras and tapes for artistic reasons, or to achieve a certain aesthetic.

- The rise of VHS in the 1980s and 1990s directly led to the creation of the video rental industry. Video stores like Blockbuster and Hollywood Video became hugely popular, with customers renting VHS tapes for a few nights at a time. *I worked at Hollywood Video for a few years, and that job helped me pay for college.*

***

BE KIND, REWIND

Blockbuster and Hollywood Video were two of the biggest players in the video rental industry during the 80s and 90s, and they've had a massive impact on our popular culture, but are also being recognized by younger kids that have gravitated to physical media.

For many people, including myself, a trip to the video store was a weekend ritual. In fact, it was an almost daily ritual after I moved out of my parents' home when I was nineteen. To this day, I love sharing the experience with the younger generation of what it was like to browse the aisles and discover new movies to rent. I remember RedBox coming out and I thought, ok, here's something somewhat close to what we grew up experiencing, but to be honest, it was just another transitional thing where technology was providing a convenience, rather than an experience.

Blockbuster and Hollywood Video were the places we went to, not just to find the next movie we were going to watch, but also to hang out, and sometimes even to talk about films with the staff or other people there that were looking for a movie to watch. For us, browsing the stacks and reading the back of vhs covers was incredibly enjoyable. Even today, I will go through the shelves of vhs tapes I own in my collection, selecting a title, and reading the description on the back cover.

This may sound comical, but some days when I went to pick out a movie at Blockbuster, if I was alone, I spent a good hour browsing the shelves in the different genres, just to see what was released and if there were movies that interested me for next time. I kept a list on a piece of paper for a long time as my "must watch" list. I wish I could remember what happened to that list!

***

THAT TIME I WORKED AT HOLLYWOOD VIDEO

Having worked at Hollywood Video in the 90s, I've been asked which video rental store I liked better back then. This is really a tough question to answer, to be honest. Like most Gen X kids, I view Blockbuster as the original big box video store that I remember having such a wonderful time in as a kid, walking the aisles and selecting the film I wanted to watch.

On the other hand, I spent a good deal of time working at Hollywood Video in my late teens, and I developed an immense love and appreciation for Hollywood Video.

I remember having lunch with a few friends and acquaintances inside a new Applebee's restaurant that just opened up. This was around 1995. I was about to graduate high school and I wanted to make money right away. Everyone was sharing what they planned to do over the summer and my best friend and I thought, why not work at Applebee's? They were hiring kitchen staff, so that made the most sense. A few of our friends mentioned working at Blockbuster or the new Hollywood Video that just opened right across from it. I thought, wow, that would really be fun, but my friend was interested in working at Applebee's, and I thought it would be great to work with him if we both got hired. We submitted applications and were hired the following week!

Funny thing, a couple of our friends began working at Blockbuster around the same time. Well, since I went to the Blockbuster to rent films, I always spent some extra time chatting with them, and I wish I could share that they had good things to say, but they didn't. Apparently, there was a tyrant manager there, and they were not really enjoying working there. It was terrible news to hear since I had cut ties with Applebee's shortly after working there because of a tyrannical supervisor and super high turnover in kitchen staff. I was searching for something new.

For a short time, I sold men's and women's shoes at Macy's (Al Bundy vibes; I know), but then came an opportunity I was not expecting. One day while searching the aisles at Hollywood video – they had one of the best foreign film collections for a video rental store – I noticed a "Now Hiring" sign. I applied, and a week later, I was the newest *Key Grip* to join the Hollywood Video team!

To say that I enjoyed working at Hollywood Video would be an understatement. I loved it! I actually wanted to go to work every single day.

Hollywood Video, like Blockbuster, was known for its vast selection of movies and TV shows, organized by genre and carefully curated by knowledgeable staff — some locations were better than others. I worked with people that loved movies as much as I did, and that was wonderful. There were quite a few perks that came along with working at Hollywood Video, including discounts on a wide range of snacks and other movie-related merchandise, as well as access to movie "screeners."

In the past, movie "screeners" played a crucial role in promoting films to video rental stores like Hollywood Video and Blockbuster. These advance copies were sent to store managers and staff, allowing us to preview upcoming releases before they hit the shelves. The intention was to generate buzz and help employees recommend titles to customers, creating a more informed rental experience. Screeners often came as VHS tapes or DVDs, sometimes lacking the final edits or special features found in retail versions. I absolutely loved screeners, and I always felt ahead of the crowd, having watched a film prior to release. I would talk the movie up to anyone walking the aisles and get patrons really hyped up about the movie.

From time to time I would connect with the friends at Blockbuster and share stories at Applebee's, ironically, and I always felt that I made the right decision about going to Hollywood Video instead of trying for Blockbuster. Plus, I got paid more!

Something we took for granted when we were younger, but that we certainly appreciate today, was that the rise of video rental stores like Blockbuster and Hollywood Video also had a significant impact on the film industry. Because movies could now be rented and watched at home, it became easier for independent and foreign films to find an audience. Filmmakers could also take risks on smaller, more unconventional projects, knowing that they could still reach a wide audience through the rental market. I watched a ton of independent and foreign films having worked at Hollywood video. I especially loved watching Akira Kurosawa samurai flicks!

Of course, the video rental industry wasn't without its controversies. There were concerns about the impact of violent or sexually explicit movies on children, and some people worried that video rental stores were contributing to the decline of movie theaters. For many people, the video store was a massive part of growing up in the 80s and 90s, and the memories of those trips to Blockbuster or Hollywood Video remain a cherished part of their childhoods.

"I believe our adventure through time has taken a most serious turn."

Ted "Theodore" Logan
(Bill & Ted's Excellent Adventure – 1989)

Chapter Ten
80S & 90s Cinema

The 1980s and 1990s were pivotal decades for cinema, shaping the tastes and memories of generations of moviegoers. However, it's impossible to comprehensively cover the vast majority of films, genres, and cultural shifts within the constraints of a single chapter. What follows is not meant to be an exhaustive analysis but rather a nostalgic journey through some of the standout moments and trends that defined these two transformative eras in cinema.

I spend a great deal of time creating content about 80s and 90s cinema on my YouTube channel, crafting retrospective documentaries on my favorite films from those decades. Movies were a huge escape for us back in the day. Before smartphones and streaming services, going to the theater was a communal event. We watched movies together, laughed together, cried together, and sometimes, we even stood in line for hours just to get tickets to the latest blockbuster. Unlike today, where binge-watching is the norm, cinema was an event—a special occasion.

I'm fully aware that this chapter only scratches the surface. I have every intention of revisiting this topic with deeper explorations in a future edition of this book. For now, consider this a love letter to the movies that shaped our collective consciousness and a promise to dive deeper in the future.

***

80S ON THE BIG SCREEN

Some of the most groundbreaking films dropped in the 80s. We had the best action blockbusters, coming-of-age stories, and romantic comedies. I dare anyone to argue that there was a better decade that produced more iconic and memorable movies in cinema history.

We had action stars like Arnold Schwarzenegger, Sylvester Stallone, Mel Gibson, Jean-Claude Van Damme, Harrison Ford, and Bruce Willis. Who can forget how amazing it was to watch *Die Hard*, *Predator*, *The Terminator*, *Rambo*, *Lethal Weapon*, or *Raiders of The Lost Ark* in theaters?

What about teen flicks? *The Breakfast Club*, *Ferris Bueller's Day Off*, *Can't Buy Me Love*, *License To Drive*, and *Say Anything*. These films captured the angst and energy of youth and remain very popular today.

What was your favorite 80s comedy flick? Here are some of mine:

- Spaceballs

- Trading Places

- Police Academy

- Three Amigos!

- Planes, Trains, and Automobiles

I haven't even mentioned sub-genre comedy films, including *Ghostbusters*, *Major League*, *Coming To America*, *Crocodile Dundee*, *Beverly Hills Cop*, *Bill & Ted's Excellent Adventure*, The Last Dragon, and *Big Trouble in Little China*.

Bill & Ted's Excellent Adventure (1989) | Orion Pictures

And can anyone deny we also had the best romantic comedies? *When Harry Met Sally, Pretty in Pink, Romancing The Stone,* and *Overboard,* just to name a few. These movies are charming, funny, and heartwarming.

The appeal of 80s cinema lies not only in the quality of the films but also in the nostalgia they evoke. For those who grew up in the 80s, these movies transport us back to a simpler time, when life was filled with big hair, neon clothing, and endless possibilities. For younger generations, these films offer a glimpse into the culture and style of a bygone era, while still resonating with universal themes that stand the test of time.

horror and science fiction movies, with filmmakers pushing the boundaries of what was possible with practical effects and exploring themes that reflected the fears and anxieties of the era.

In the horror genre, the 80s saw the rise of the slasher film, with franchises like *Halloween, Friday the 13th,* and *A Nightmare on Elm Street* becoming cultural touchstones. These films often featured masked or supernatural killers preying on teenagers, and while they were criticized for their graphic violence and gratuitous nudity, they were also celebrated for their suspenseful storytelling and creative use of gore effects.

But horror in the 80s wasn't just about slashers. Filmmakers like David Cronenberg and Clive Barker brought a more cerebral and psychological approach to horror with films like *The Fly* and *Hellraiser,* which explored body horror and the dark corners of the human psyche.

In the science fiction genre, we watched blockbuster films like *Star Wars, E.T. the Extra-Terrestrial,* and the *Back to the Future* trilogy, which combined thrilling action and adventure with cutting-edge special effects and relatable characters. These films appealed to audiences of all ages and spawned a legion of sequels, spin-offs, and imitators.

But the 80s also saw a wave of darker, more dystopian sci-fi films, like *Blade Runner*, *The Terminator*, and *RoboCop*, which imagined bleak, violent futures and questioned the morality of technology and artificial intelligence.

I remember watching *RoboCop* for the first time and how shocked I was during the violent murder of officer Alex Murphy (Peter Weller). The 80s didn't hold back!

***

90S ON THE BIG SCREEN

A more serious and introspective approach to filmmaking characterized 90s films. Directors like Quentin Tarantino and Kevin Smith emerged during this time, bringing their unique perspective to storytelling and exploring themes like violence, crime, comedy, and identity in new and provocative ways.

One of the biggest changes in cinema during the 90s was the rise of independent filmmaking. As the cost of making films came down, more and more filmmakers could make movies outside of the Hollywood studio system. This led to a wave of innovative and thought invoking films like *Pulp Fiction*, *Clerks*, and *Boyz n the Hood*.

Some unforgettable films that defined the decade include:

THE BLOCKBUSTERS THAT BLEW OUR MINDS

- *Jurassic Park* (where CGI finally met its match in Jeff Goldblum's charisma)
- *The Matrix* (blue pill or red pill?)
- *Terminator 2* (proving that even killer cyborg can learn to feel)

FANTASTIC DRAMAS

- *The Shawshank Redemption* (teaching us that hope is always worth having)

- *Good Will Hunting* (how do you like them apples?)

- *Forrest Gump* (life is indeed like a box of chocolates)

THE FILMS THAT KEPT US UP AT NIGHT

- *The Silence of The Lambs* (fava beans, anyone?)

- *Seven* (what's in the box? NO, REALLY, WHAT'S IN THE BOX?)

- *Scream* (pass on answering the phone)

HILARIOUS COMEDIES THAT STILL MAKE US LAUGH

- *There's Something About Mary* (hair gel will never be the same)

- *Dumb and Dumber* (so stupid it's brilliant)

- *Romy and Michele's High School Reunion* (because Post-It notes ARE a valid business claim)

THE HIDDEN GEMS

- *Desperado* (Antonio Banderas with a guitar case full of guns – need I say more?)

- *Tombstone* (I'm your huckleberry)

- *Leon: The Professional* (young Natalie Portman stealing scenes from everyone)

Despite the differences stylistically between the two decades, the 80s and 90s shared a very important similarity— Culturally, they were both marked by a growing influence of youth culture, with films often centered on teenage protagonists navigating their identities– think movies like *The Breakfast Club* (1985) or Kevin Smith's highly underrated film, *Chasing Amy* (1997).

Finally, both decades were shaped by significant musical influences, with iconic soundtracks that not only complemented the films but also became a huge part of why we became fond of the films— think, *Purple Rain* (1984) and *Armageddon* (1998). And what about *Singles* (basically a love letter to grunge)?

***

When I'm searching for a movie to watch, I usually dig into my 80s and 90s archive before checking what's streaming. There's a unique charm and cinematic quality to the films of these decades that modern movies rarely replicate. The warmth of nostalgia and the comfort of revisiting old favorites keep pulling me back. And perhaps that's the magic of these movies—they're not just films to me—they're time machines.

Day of The Outlaw (1959) Theatrical Release Poster

I've observed that my father has been rewatching many of the Westerns he grew up seeing as a kid in the 1960s and 1970s. Last week I got a chance to view *Day of The Outlaw*, a 1959 film about a cattleman that feuds with the small community he helped found in Bitters, Wyoming. While I found the story compelling, and certainly enjoyed watching Tina Louise before her famous role as Ginger Grant on *Gilligan's Island*, I was unimpressed with the sets and the acting. The film was dated. I think my dad was also conscious of just how far Western films have come, especially after we started watching 3:10 To Yuma (2007) right after. By the way, check out the original 3:10 To Yuma (1957). It's a great film. However, the 2007 version will still seem like it was only recently produced fifty years from now.

Western films are a great case study in movie making and period piece setting. When I compare the film to a modest budget western from the 1980s, like *The Long Riders* (1980), there's just no comparison. It's incredible how much the stage settings, direction, acting, and film processing had changed in about a twenty year period. By the time *Pale Rider* (1985), *Silverado* (1985), *Young Guns* (1989), *Dances with Wolves* (1990), *Unforgiven* (1992), and *Tombstone* (1993) were made, the western genre had matured leaps and bounds. The difference now is that the westerns from the 1980s and 1990s have not lost their luster whatsoever. I recall my oldest son and I catching *Tombstone* (1993) streaming a short time ago and he asked me if the film just came out! That's a testament to the "feel" of films from the 80s and 90s. He would have never said that about a film like Day of The Outlaw.

Tombstone VHS Tape (1994)

Speaking of western films, I grew up watching Clint Eastwood movies. Although early Eastwood Westerns may seem dated, they were incredibly more enjoyable to watch than Westerns made ten or twenty years before them — I'm talking 60s and 70s Eastwood Westerns. My point is, the 1980s represented a significant period where technological advancements, storytelling and acting, and filmmaking techniques converged to create a transformative and immortal era in cinema.

This chapter is just the beginning of a conversation I hope to expand upon in future works. The 80s and 90s were rich, vibrant, and endlessly fascinating periods for cinema. Let this be an invitation to revisit the films you love and rediscover the joy they brought to your life.

VHS Tapes from my personal collection

"Of all the Basic Applied Economic Principles of Capitalism in the Post-Industrial Era Seminars in the world, you had to walk into mine."

Michael J. Fox as Alex P. Keaton
(Family Ties - 1982 to 1989)

Chapter Eleven
Prime-Time Nostalgia

When Cable Was Still Optional

Remember when we actually had to be home at a specific time to watch our favorite shows? The 1980s were the last great era of appointment television, when our families would gather around that wood-paneled console TV to watch the same show together – whether or not we wanted to.

When I post about a show on social media, it's really incredible the similarities in comments that my post receives. I think one of the strongest forces that binds us as Gen Xers is the fact we shared our television memories every day across the country, and the only difference was the time zone.

Prime-Time television shows glued us to the tv set, and it didn't matter what your day was like, after dinner, you could sit in the same room together and enjoy a great program together. Not so much today, right? There are so many options today, including competing entertainment options like creator channels on YouTube. The shared appointment television experience has disappeared, unfortunately.

Let's explore some of my favorite shows from the 80s that I'm sure you watched and enjoyed as well:

The Cosby Show

The Bill Cosby Show | Hartford Courant TV WEEK Issue (1984)

Thursday nights belonged to the Huxtables, period. We watched a successful Black family navigate life with wit, style, and an endless parade of terrible sweaters. The show was groundbreaking for its time, presenting an upper-middle-class African American family when most TV executives thought audiences wouldn't relate. Turns out, everyone could relate to trying to hide bad report cards from their parents and awkward teenage dating moments. Of course, now it's practically impossible to watch reruns of The Cosby show without feeling deeply uncomfortable, proving once again that Gen X can't have nice things.

RAD FACT:

The Cosby Show was the highest-rated sitcom for five consecutive seasons and is credited with reviving the sitcom genre.

Cheers

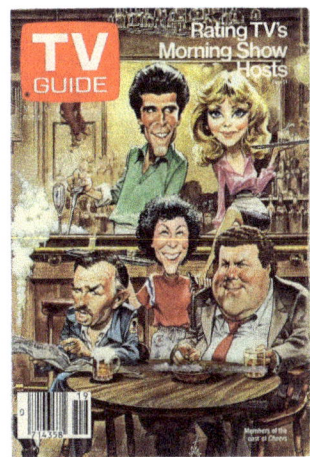

CHEERS CAST, BRUCE STARK ART | TV GUIDE (MAY 1986)

Where everybody knows your name – unless you're trying to get into an actual Boston bar, in which case good luck with that *pahking* situation. This show about a bar full of lovable misfits gave us the greatest "will they/won't they" relationship in TV history with Sam and Diane until Shelley Long pursued a film career that peaked with "Troop Beverly Hills." The show survived her departure, though, which is more than we can say for most of our parents' marriages in the '80s.

RAD FACT:

Cheers won 28 Emmy Awards and was named one of the greatest TV–shows of all time by TV GUIDE.

Family Ties

FAMILY TIES | TV GUIDE Issue (APR 1985)

Alex P. Keaton was every conservative parent's dream and every hippie parent's nightmare. Michael J. Fox turned a young Republican in a suit into someone actually likable – a feat perhaps more impressive than time traveling in a DeLorean. The show captured the exact moment when 60s idealism crashed headlong into 80s materialism, and somehow made both sides look equally ridiculous. Plus, it gave us one of TV's greatest drug PSAs with Tom Hanks as Uncle Ned. Sha-la-la-la.

RAD FACT:

Sit Ubu, Sit. "Sit, Ubu, Sit" was a production company logo used at the end of the closing credits for the television show "Family Ties." The words are accompanied by a visual of a black Labrador Retriever sitting in profile with a frisbee in its mouth. The dog's real name was Ubu Roi, and he belonged to the series creator Gary David Goldberg and his family.

Miami Vice

MIAMI VICE | TV GUIDE Issue (JULY 1985)

The show that convinced an entire generation that pastels and no socks were a legitimate fashion choice. Crockett and Tubbs fought crime in a Ferrari Daytona Spider and Ferrari Testarossa while Phil Collins and Jan Hammer provided the soundtrack to every drug bust. The show was pure style! It was the first TV show to look like an MTV video, which made perfect sense since half the budget went to music rights and the other half to Don Johnson's wardrobe!

RAD FACT:

1. *Miami Vice* was one of the first TV shows to use top-tier, chart-topping music as a central storytelling tool. Phil Collins, Glenn Frey, and U2 all made their way into episodes. The licensing costs for music alone were astronomical, with up to $10,000 per episode being spent on music rights—a fortune in the 1980s! This gamble paid off, turning the show into a massive hit.

Knight Rider

Knight Rider, VROOM! | TV Magazine Ad (1982)

A man and his talking car fight crime. That's it. That's the show. And we LOVED it. KITT was Siri before Siri existed, except KITT had an actual personality and wouldn't accidentally order you 20 pizzas. Looking back, David Hasselhoff's Michael Knight spent an awful lot of time having deep conversations with his car, but then again, who among us hasn't named their vehicle and talked to it? The funny thing is our watches can now communicate with not only our vehicles but also our homes!

RAD FACT:

The voice of KITT, William Daniels, was so in demand that he recorded his lines *without ever meeting* David Hasselhoff during the show's original run. Also, KITT's flashy red scanner light was inspired by the Cylons from *Battlestar Galactica*, another Glen A. Larson creation. Proof that even in the '80s, good ideas got recycled—just like those endless turbo-boost stunts.

The A-Team

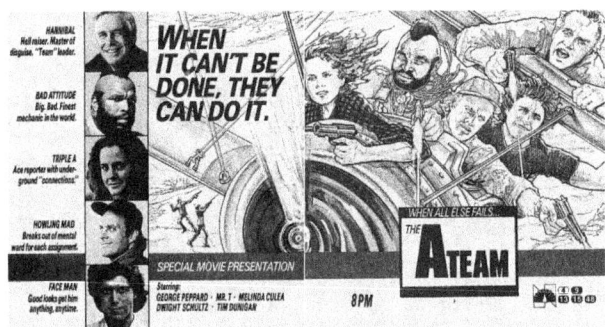

The A-Team | TV GUIDE Debut Insert (JAN 1983)

If you had a problem, if no one else could help, and if you could find them, you could hire four Vietnam vets who somehow never kill anyone despite firing approximately 30,000 rounds per episode. Mr. T became everyone's favorite mohawked role model, teaching us to pity fools and drink our milk. The A-Team built more improbable weapons out of random junk than all of MacGyver's episodes combined, yet never seemed to run out of conveniently placed welding tools in abandoned warehouses.

RAD FACT:

The legendary black-and-red GMC Vandura wasn't just a set piece—it was *the* mobile HQ. While it became a cultural icon, driving it was less glamorous. Cast members joked about how cramped and bumpy it was, especially for long shoots. But hey, it sure looked cool crashing through barricades!

Magnum, P.I.

Magnum P.I. | TV GUIDE Ad (NOV 1981)

Magnum, P.I. is my favorite 80s show as an adult. Tom Selleck's mustache starred as a private investigator in Hawaii, with Tom Selleck himself in a supporting role. Magnum solved crimes while living rent-free in a mansion, driving a Ferrari he didn't own, and wearing the shortest shorts known to man. It was basically a masterclass in failing upward, and we loved it. The show also taught me you could make a living as a private investigator in Hawaii while only doing about 15 minutes of actual work per episode.

RAD FACT:

1. Tom Selleck's iconic mustache almost didn't make it onto the show! Producers originally wanted Magnum to be clean-shaven, but Selleck insisted on keeping the 'stache—and it quickly became one of the most famous facial hair statements of the 80s.

MacGyver

MacGyver Print Ad (1986)

The show that launched a thousand science fair projects and convinced an entire generation that they, too, could defuse a nuclear bomb with a paperclip and some chewing gum. Richard Dean Anderson's mullet deserved its own credit in the opening sequence, and the show made science cool before being a nerd was socially acceptable. MacGyver was like James Bond if Q had gone on strike and 007 had to shop at Radio Shack.

RAD FACT:

MacGyver turned duct tape, paperclips, and chewing gum into tools of espionage. Richard Dean Anderson's character avoided guns, making him the ultimate pacifist action hero. The show's writers even hired a physicist to ensure MacGyver's DIY gadgets were *somewhat* plausible, though many were still more Hollywood magic than science fair project.

Dallas

Dallas, Who Shot J.R.! | TV GUIDE Clipping (NOV 1980)

The show with one of the greatest cliffhangers ever! It launched "Who Shot J.R.?" t-shirts and made shoulder pads a requirement for doing business in Texas. Dallas was basically a soap opera with bigger hair and oil wells, proving that rich people's problems are just like regular people's problems, except with more helicopters and ranch houses. The show's infamous "it was all a dream" season remains the ultimate cop-out in television history – something we're still not over.

RAD FACT:

Although *Dallas* was set in the Lone Star State, most of the series was filmed in Los Angeles. Only a few iconic exteriors, like Southfork Ranch, were actually shot in Texas. But thanks to oil wells, big hair, and Southern drawls, viewers bought the Texas fantasy hook, line, and sinker.

Airwolf

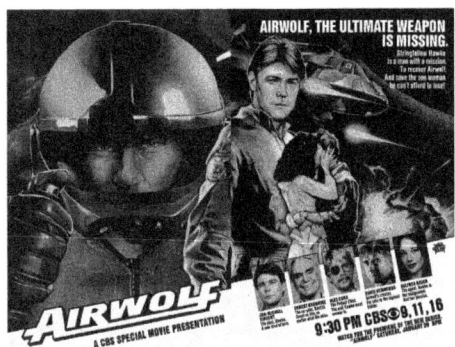

Airwolf | TV GUIDE Debut Insert (JAN 1984)

Because one show about a high-tech vehicle fighting crime wasn't enough, we also had Airwolf – basically Knight Rider with a helicopter. Jan-Michael Vincent and Ernest Borgnine flew around in what was essentially a stealth helicopter. The show existed in that sweet spot of 80s television where the Cold War was still a thing, but we could solve it with cool vehicles and synthesizer music.

RAD FACT:

The titular Airwolf helicopter wasn't just a cool TV prop—it was a heavily modified Bell 222, tricked out with a sleek black-and-silver paint job. In reality, the helicopter didn't have weapons or supersonic speed, but it sure looked like it could outfly anything on screen. The show's producers even reused stock footage of Airwolf in action to save on production costs—because making a chopper look that cool wasn't cheap!

Growing Pains

GROWING PAINS | TV GUIDE Clipping (SEP 1985)

Show me that smile again...

I absolutely loved Growing Pains! The show was a weekly reminder that even functional families could be wonderfully dysfunctional. Every character was relatable! The Seavers somehow nailed that sweet spot between The Brady Bunch perfection and Married with Children chaos. Jason Seaver was the world's most available psychiatrist, running his practice from home yet somehow never seeming to actually see patients.

Maggie gave us the revolutionary concept of a working mom who didn't need to apologize for her career, even if the show rarely showed her at work either. And then there was Kirk Cameron as Mike Seaver, the lovable underachiever who made getting C's look cool and turned "sitting backwards in a chair while delivering wisecracks" into an art form. The show gave us classic episodes like Mike hiring a homeless teen (played by a young Brad Pitt) to be his tutor, Carol's eating disorder, and Ben's endless schemes that proved being the middle child really is a thing.

Early Growing Pains captured that perfect 80s family sitcom vibe where problems were solved with heart-to-hearts in roughly 22 minutes, usually while someone was sitting on someone else's bed.

The show's theme song promised to show us that smile again, and honestly, it delivered every single time.

Perfect Strangers

Perfect Strangers 3" Pinback Button (1986)

Cousins Larry and Balki taught us that if you do the Dance of Joy enough times, everything will work out fine. Bronson Pinchot's Balki Bartokomous made "Don't be ridiculous!" the catch phrase of choice for anyone who couldn't quite nail his Mypos accent (which was everyone). The show was basically a buddy comedy that asked the important question: What if your cousin from a made-up Mediterranean country moved in with you and refused to understand basic American customs?

I rewatched the entire series earlier this year with my wife, who was watching it for the first time, and was amazed at just how funny the show still was. My wife absolutely loved the series, and it was a real joy to experience the show through her laughter.

RAD FACT:

The "Dance of Joy" - one of the show's most memorable running gags - was actually created by accident during rehearsals! One day, Bronson Pinchot and Mark Linn-Baker were goofing around between takes and started doing this silly, spontaneous celebratory dance. The producers saw it and loved it so much they wrote it into the show.

The Wonder Years

The Wonder Years | TV GUIDE Inserts (1988-93)

Nothing captured suburban Gen X childhood quite like Kevin Arnold's coming-of-age story, narrated by Daniel Stern's voice of regret. The show made us all feel like our awkward school experiences and first crushes were profound and meaningful instead of just embarrassing. Winnie Cooper became everyone's ideal first love, while Paul Pfeiffer became everyone's actual first friend. And let's be honest – we all tried to perfect that Fred Savage side-eye at some point.

RAD FACT:

1. *The Wonder Years* featured Joe Cocker's soulful cover of "With a Little Help from My Friends" as its theme song, but the show had trouble securing other Beatles tracks. Rights issues meant some songs were replaced in home video releases, making the original broadcasts even more special for fans who heard the authentic soundtrack.

2. Fred Savage (Kevin) and Josh Saviano (Paul Pfeiffer) weren't just buddies on screen—they became lifelong friends off screen too. Fans have long speculated about Paul's adult life, with one of the most popular rumors being that he grew up to become Marilyn Manson (he didn't). In reality, Saviano became a successful lawyer.

Who's the Boss?

Who's the Boss Promotional Lobby Card

A former baseball player becomes a housekeeper in Connecticut, and somehow this premise sustained eight seasons. Tony Danza played Tony Micelli, shocking audiences by proving that yes, he could play a character named Tony. The real star was Judith Light's Angela, showing us that career women could have it all— if "all" meant a good-looking housekeeper and a mother who talked about sex way too much. The show asked "Who's the Boss?" but never really answered it.

RAD FACTS:

1. Like their characters, Tony Danza and Alyssa Milano are from Brooklyn in real life.

2. TV Guide tipped their hat to Tony Micelli in their Father's Day special issue (2004). In their roundup of television's most memorable dads, Danza's portrayal of the devoted single father landed at #23 - pretty impressive considering the decades of TV fathers in contention!

Moonlighting

Moonlighting | Newsweek Magazine (SEP 1986)

Before Bruce Willis was yippee-ki-yaying his way through Die Hard, he was trading razor-sharp banter with Cybill Shepherd in this detective series that was part romance, part comedy, and all sexual tension. The show was famous for breaking the fourth wall before breaking the fourth wall was cool, and for having production delays that would make George R.R. Martin feel punctual. It also proved that TV couples should never, ever get together, a lesson that future shows would repeatedly ignore.

RAD FACT:

When Maddie and David finally got together, it sparked what fans call the "Moonlighting Curse." The show's famously sizzling "will-they-won't-they" tension fizzled after their romance became official. Many credit this dynamic shift with the show's eventual decline — a lesson in keeping the spark alive by keeping it just out of reach.

Silver Spoons

Silver Spoons | TV GUIDE (May 1983)

Ricky Schroder lived every kid's dream: a mansion full of toys, including an actual train that ran through the house. His man-child father taught us that being rich meant never having to grow up, while we all wondered how a toy company could generate that much wealth. The show gave us early glimpses of Jason Bateman and Alfonso Ribeiro before they went on to their more famous roles, proving that even silver spoons need a backup plan.

The show was pure wealth fantasy for Reagan-era kids, giving us a mansion full of video games and toys while teaching us heartwarming lessons about responsibility. Silver Spoons was one of my favorite shows. Being a poor kid in the 80s made you wonder if people actually lived like this on tv. As an adult, I've found that the show was not far off from how the wealthy live.

As I think back to 80s television and just how glued I was to it, it's crazy to think that the 80s were the last gasp of unified popular culture, before cable TV exploded and the internet fractured our attention spans into a million pieces. Now we can stream any show we want, anytime we want, but something's missing. Maybe it's the anticipation of waiting an entire week for a new episode. Maybe it's the shared experience of everyone watching the same thing at the same time. Or maybe we just miss the simplicity of a world where all problems could be solved in 48 minutes (minus commercials), preferably with a montage set to power ballads.

Star Trek: The Next Generation

 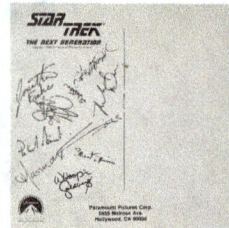

Star Trek Next Generation Cast Autographed Postcard | Paramount Pictures (1988)

Make it so! Patrick Stewart's Jean-Luc Picard proved that bald is beautiful and that Shakespeare in space totally works. TNG gave us technobabble that actually sounded plausible, uniforms that looked uncomfortable as hell, and a ship's counselor who basically just stated the obvious while wearing increasingly questionable outfits (Deanna Troi). The show tackled serious issues while Data tried to understand humans, which is still more success than most of us have had with that task. I loved this show. It had everything, really. It also made us think. The characters were all relatable and the conflict between the different factions was always set to stun. One of the many things I loved about Star Trek: The Next Generation was the amazing ship designs, especially the Romulan Warbird.

RAD FACT:

Patrick Stewart initially passed on the role of Captain Jean-Luc Picard. He didn't think the character would be compelling enough. After reading the script, Stewart was hooked, and he soon became one of the most beloved captains in *Star Trek* history!

Quantum Leap

Quantum Leap | TV GUIDE Teaser

Oh boy! Scott Bakula's Dr. Sam Beckett ping-ponged through time, trying to put right what once went wrong, while we all pretended to understand how the entire process worked. His holographic guide Al (Dean Stockwell) provided fashion choices that were wrong even by 80s standards. The show taught us that history could be changed by one person, as long as that person had a super-computer named Ziggy and a friend with a light-up handset.

RAD FACT:

During the show's run, Scott Bakula actually performed all of his own songs and piano playing scenes - he was an accomplished Broadway musician before taking the role of Sam Beckett. This talent came in especially handy in episodes where Sam leaped into musicians!

The Golden Girls

The Golden Girls Kitchen Filming Set

The show that proved four sassy women and a lanai could be the ultimate weapon against boredom. *The Golden Girls* took the sitcom world by storm, convincing an entire generation that cheesecake and savage one-liners were the only way to settle a debate. With Blanche's scandalous escapades, Dorothy's epic burns, Rose's St. Olaf ramblings, and Sophia's ability to roast everyone within a ten-foot radius, this show didn't just have heart—it had a mouth.

RAD FACT:

The iconic kitchen table had just three chairs instead of four to make the scenes easier to shoot. That meant someone was *always* sitting out on the lanai, plotting their next zinger.

***

FORGOTTEN CULT CLASSICS

The Shows That Time (Mostly) Forgot

Every decade has its standout television shows. The 1980s were a unique decade, with programs that were high-concept but limited by low production budgets, or shows that embraced their ridiculousness so fully that they became cult classics. These less-appreciated shows hold a special place in our hearts. In fact, if I mention one of these shows in casual conversation and someone recognizes it, I know we're going to be fast friends!

Manimal

Manimal | TV GUIDE Insert

Because someone in a pitch meeting actually said, "What if we had a dashing British professor who could turn into any animal to fight crime?" and instead of being laughed out of the room, they got a green light. Dr. Jonathan Chase could transform into animals at will, though apparently, they only had enough budget to turn him into a hawk or a black panther most of the time. The transformation sequences were done by master makeup artist Stan Winston, which was like hiring Picasso to paint your garage. The show had all the subtlety of a gorilla at a tea party, with our hero regularly choosing to turn into a panther in broad daylight on busy New York streets because... for no reason.

RAD FACTS:

1. Stan Winston's transformation sequences cost so much that they had to reuse them in multiple episodes.

2. Star Simon MacCorkindale had to sit through 4 hours of makeup for trans-

formations that lasted seconds on screen.

Automan

Automan | TV GUIDE Insert

Imagine Tron had a baby with Knight Rider, raised by Chuck. A police computer expert creates a holographic superhero who steps out of the computer to fight crime, accompanied by his floating geometric sidekick Cursor. Automan could create any vehicle he needed by having Cursor draw it (in perfect neon blue, naturally), but only operated at night because his programs used too much electricity. This was basically "my computer crashed" taken to a whole new level.

RAD FACTS:

1. The glowing suit worn by Chuck Wagner actually ran on car batteries and cost $100,000 to make.

2. Glen A. Larson, the same guy who gave us **Knight Rider** and **Battlestar Galactica** created the show.

3. They had to film in the dark for all *Automan* scenes because the suit

wouldn't show up properly otherwise

My Secret Identity

My Secret Identity Book | Scholastic - Jovial Bob Stine (1989)

Jerry O'Connell starred as a teenager who gets zapped by a photon beam and gains superpowers, because the 80s taught us that radiation gives you cool abilities instead of cancer. He could fly by using aerosol cans as propulsion, which simultaneously destroyed the ozone layer and every kid's allowance as they wasted entire cans of hairspray trying to hover (I actually tried this). The show was basically Greatest American Hero for the Tiger Beat crowd, minus the cool suit but plus a lot more teenage awkwardness.

Speaking of Jerry O'Connell, he might be the most versatile Gen X actor you've never properly appreciated. From his memorable breakout role as the pudgy Vern Tessio in Stand By Me to his transformation into a leading man in Sliders, O'Connell has quietly built one of the most sustainable careers in Hollywood.

Unlike many child actors who peaked early, he successfully navigated the treacherous waters from teen heartthrob to legitimate adult actor, somehow managing to skip the obligatory tabloid meltdown phase entirely. He's a versatile actor too. His ability to bounce between drama (Jerry Maguire), horror (Scream 2), and comedy (Joe's Apartment) speaks to a range that's been consistently overlooked by critics.

In 2021, O'Connell reinvented himself yet again as a daytime TV personality, co-hosting The Talk with an effortless charm. As I write this book, the show is in its 15th and final season on CBS. His marriage to Rebecca Romijn, while notable, has never overshadowed his own career— a rarity in Hollywood relationships.

Perhaps what makes O'Connell so quintessentially Gen X is how he's managed to stay relevant without ever seeming to try too hard, maintaining a career longevity that many of his more celebrated peers would envy.

RAD FACTS:

1. My Secret Identity ran for three seasons in Canada before most American audiences ever saw it.

2. The special effects budget was so low they often used reverse footage of O'Connell jumping to show him landing from flight.

Voyagers!

Voyagers! | *TV GUIDE Story*
(SEP 1982)

Time travel was never more educational or fashion-conscious than with Phineas Bogg and Jeffrey Jones, who bounced through history fixing things that got screwed up, like a temporal AAA service. Bogg was a time traveler who looked like he raided Fabio's closet, while Jeffrey was a kid who knew more about history than the actual time traveler (because that makes sense). They used a device called an Omni that looked suspiciously like a pocket watch with Christmas lights. I only wish it lasted longer. The show was canceled after the show's star, Jon-Erik Hexum, tragically died in 1984 from an accident with a prop gun on.

RAD FACTS:

1. The original concept had Bogg traveling alone until someone realized adding a kid would help attract younger viewers.

2. The show's educational content helped it fulfill NBC's educational programming requirements.

Beauty and the Beast

Above And Below: A Guide To Beauty And The Beast (1990)

No singing teapots here - just Ron Perlman in amazing makeup wooing Linda Hamilton in a weird romantic fantasy set in the tunnels beneath New York City. Vincent (the Beast) read classical poetry and quoted literature while ripping bad guys apart, proving that an English degree can be useful in combat. The show somehow made the New York sewers look romantic, which is a feat deserving of an Emmy all by itself.

RAD FACTS:

1. Ron Perlman spent 3 hours every day in makeup.

2. George R.R. Martin was a writer and producer for the show.

3. Actual communities living in NYC's abandoned subway tunnels inspired the show's underground world.

Sledge Hammer!

Sledge Hammer | TV GUIDE Insert

Before The Naked Gun and Hot Shots, there was Sledge Hammer, a parody of Dirty Harry-type cops that was way ahead of its time. David Rasche played the trigger-happy detective who talked to his gun, slept with his gun, and probably would have married his gun if California law had allowed it. The show ended its first season when Hammer accidentally destroys the city when he attempts to disarm a stolen nuclear warhead. The show was renewed unexpectedly for a second season.

RAD FACTS:

1. The show's creator, Alan Spencer, wrote the pilot at age 16.

2. Hammer's gun was a .44 Magnum with *I love you* engraved on it.

3. The first season finale literally nuked San Francisco because they thought they were being canceled.

The Greatest American Hero

The Greatest American Hero | TV GUIDE Promo

Believe it or not, this show about a teacher who gets a super suit from aliens but loses the instruction manual was actually kind of brilliant. It also happens to be my favorite cult classic TV show on this list! William Katt's Ralph Hinkley (later changed to Hanley after the John Hinckley Jr. assassination attempt on Reagan) spent more time crashing into walls than actually flying, which is honestly what would happen if any of us got super powers and lost the instructions. Paired with rigid FBI agent Bill Maxwell (Robert Culp) and understanding girlfriend Pam Davidson (Connie Sellecca), Ralph bumbled his way through saving the world while trying to grade papers and keep his students from discovering his secret.

The show gave us some genuinely great episodes. The pilot was a wonderful episode that sucked you right in. Another favorite episode of mine was Operation Spoilsport. In this episode, the aliens come back to warn Ralph that a failsafe system designed to prevent retaliation against the enemy has malfunctioned. As a result, the world is on high alert, facing the imminent threat of World War III.

The real magic was in how the show embraced its own ridiculousness. Ralph never really mastered the suit's powers, turning every rescue into a comedy of errors that somehow worked out. He'd attempt to land gracefully and end up face-first in a cactus, try to use super-strength and accidentally launch something into orbit, or attempt invisibility only to have just his clothes disappear. And let's not forget that theme song - Joey Scarbury's Believe It or Not spent more weeks on the Billboard Hot 100 than the show spent on air, becoming the earworm that launched a thousand karaoke fails.

RAD FACTS:

1. Stephen J. Cannell wrote the pilot in just one day.

2. The suit was intentionally made too small for William Katt to make him look more awkward.

3. Test audiences found the original pilot too serious, leading to the more comedic tone.

4. Robert Culp wrote several episodes of the series himself

***

These shows represent the beautiful creativity (insanity) of 80s television, when network executives were apparently willing to green-light almost anything as long as it had either a supernatural element, a computer, or a guy in weird makeup. While they may not have lasted long, we still remember and love them. Just how much coke were these executives doing back in the 80s?

"Everyone has a plan until they get punched in the face."

Mike Tyson

© *Nintendo*

Chapter Twelve

The Golden Age of Sports?

Nostalgia, Progress, and the Evolving Game

One thing I appreciate is how convenient it is to watch sports now. I also enjoy the convenience of sports apps and having game scores and highlights at my fingertips. But I have to admit, there was a certain charm to the simpler times, when athletes seemed more grounded and the focus was solely on the game. Sports leagues, owners, franchises, and athletes have become more political and far too social over the years. So much so that the on-and-off the field activities have become a distraction. I remember when the absence of the pervasive social and political commentary that often dominates modern sports discourse allowed fans to simply enjoy the competition.

Still, we can't discount the significant strides that have been made in the world of sports. The advancements in technology, from close-ups and replays, the high-definition television, to advanced analytics– these things have revolutionized the way we consume and understand sports. For example, one of my favorite things to do is to watch the *NFL Red Zone* channel, which offers an unparalleled level of access and insight, and I'm basically tapped into the entire NFL network of games on Sundays.

And yet, even when we didn't have instant highlights or hot take influencers screaming at us 24/7 on social media, I feel like we appreciated sports more. I get it– we watched the action through fuzzy TV reception, read the newspaper box scores, and had playground debates that could never be settled by a quick Google search, but there was something special about having the same shared experience– it allowed us to think for ourselves.

Famous 1980s Sports Illustrated Covers from My collection

There's no doubt the 1980s were our coming-of-age decade in sports, and looking back, we witnessed some of the most iconic moments in history—even if we had to adjust the antenna to see them clearly.

The decade kicked off with the moment that made us believe in miracles. On February 22, 1980, a bunch of college kids took down the mighty Soviet Union hockey machine in Lake Placid. Even those of us who cared little about hockey understood what it meant when Al Michaels asked us if we believed in miracles. The *Miracle on Ice* was Cold War theater played out on ice!

1980 also gave us the birth of CNN and ESPN. CNN was for our parents to obsess over world events, but ESPN? That was ours. I didn't start watching ESPN fairly regularly until the mid-80s, but I was hooked as the network became more refined. Before ESPN became the worldwide leader in manufactured debate around sports, it was just a scrappy cable channel showing whatever sports they could afford the rights to. Sometimes, it felt like they were just making things up as they went along. It was kind of hilarious, actually.

The NFL provided us with a moment that showed defense can be just as thrilling as offense. For me and many others, the 1985 Chicago Bears are synonymous with nostalgia. The *Super Bowl Shuffle* was so gloriously cheesy that it could only have happened in the 80s, and we ate it up. The Bears' 46 Defense, led by Mike Singletary's intense stare and William "Refrigerator" Perry's unlikely touchdown runs, showed us that football could be both brutal and fun. They demolished the Patriots 46-10 in Super Bowl XX, and even non-Bears fans had to admit there was something special about watching a 300-pound defensive lineman score touchdowns. Now I was, and still am, a Detroit Lions fan, but that '85 Bears team was something else.

*Chicago Bears Super Bowl Shuffle 12" Vinyl
(1985) with K-Mart Sticker*

But let's talk about the man who redefined what was possible in sports—Michael Jordan. We watched him evolve from the skinny kid from North Carolina who hit the game-winner in the 1982 NCAA Championship to His Airness. The 1988 Slam Dunk Contest, where he took off from the free-throw line (twice!) was pure magic. That same year, he won his first MVP award and Defensive Player of the Year. Think about that—the most explosive offensive player in the game was also its best defender. Jordan didn't just change basketball; he changed how we thought about athletic excellence. For the record, he is the greatest basketball player of all time. Sorry Kobe and Lebron fans.

Baseball gave us enough drama for a dozen soap operas. Game 6 of the 1986 World Series between the Mets and Red Sox taught us about tragedy and redemption. When Bill Buckner let that ground ball roll through his legs, we learned that one moment could haunt you forever. That he was actually a great player for 22 seasons didn't matter — he became defined by a single error. That's some heavy stuff to process when you're growing up. The first World Series I really ever remember, just because I was so invested in the game as a kid from Detroit, was the 1984 World Series. This series featured the Detroit Tigers vs the San Diego Padres. The Tigers, along with Kirk Gibson aka "Mr. Clutch," Alan Trammell, and Willie Hernandez, won the World Series that year. Oh, and there were celebratory riots in Detroit after The Tigers won, which no respectful resident of

Detroit can forget. The real irony though is that I've been a Padres fan since moving to San Diego in 1989!

The steroid era was just beginning to rear its muscled head in the late 80s, though we didn't know it then. We were too busy watching Wade Boggs hit .350 every year and Rickey Henderson steal bases like crazy. Henderson broke Lou Brock's all-time stolen base record in 1991, and the buildup to that was something to behold. Every time Henderson got on base, everything stopped. We didn't need a pitch clock because we had Rickey messing with pitchers' heads.

1991 Upper Deck Rickey Henderson #444 Baseball Card

***

A note on steroids in baseball:

The steroid era is arguably the most exciting time in baseball history. One of my favorite things to do during the late 80s and into the 90s was to watch sports with my best friend. We especially loved baseball because we collected baseball cards. We tracked statistics, and we loved tracking home runs– So did everyone else. Some of our favorite baseball players to watch included Mark McGwire, Barry Bonds, Sammy Sosa, Rafael Palmeiro, Jose Canseco, Jason Giambi, Gary Sheffield, Miguel Tejada, Manny Ramirez, Alex Rodriguez, and Roger Clemens. Sadly, these athletes were embroiled in the steroid inquisition. Steroid use among professional athletes is a recurring issue, and its continued presence and growth are evidenced by the many athletes linked to its use over the years. You would be surprised, or maybe not, that even to this day, professional athletes cycle on and off of steroids, having apparent knowledge of when testing will happen. Unfortunately, some of our most beloved and talented baseball players will never be recognized in the Hall of Fame because they were labeled as "bad guys" to appease public opinion. This has always been frustrating for me and many baseball fans from my generation. I suppose what I'd like to see is the players inducted into the Hall of Fame with an asterisk next to their names at the very least.

***

Ok, let's talk boxing, because it was peak drama in the 80s and 90s! That said, it was also the realest boxing has been since the early 2000s. Have you tried watching boxing today? It's an absolute travesty what's happened to the sport!

My dad and I used to bond over boxing. Some of my fondest memories are of my dad and I watching boxing matches together. Just check out some of these great fights: Sugar Ray Leonard vs Marvelous Marvin Hagler, Sugar Ray Leonard vs Thomas "Hitman" Hearns, Larry Holmes vs Gerry Cooney, Marvelous Marvin Hagler vs Roberto Duran, and pretty much any match where Mike Tyson, George Foreman, or Evander Holyfield were fighting.

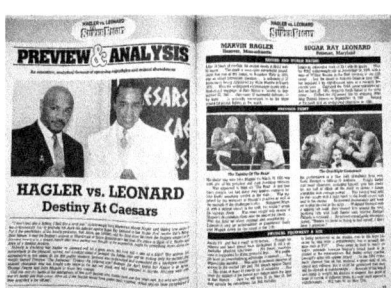

World Boxing Magazine | Sugar Ray Leonard Vs. Marvin Hagler Preview Section (May 1987)

Mike Tyson emerged like something out of a comic book. He was a 19-year-old wrecking ball who made grown men look like they'd rather be anywhere else. We watched him unify the heavyweight titles and become the youngest heavyweight champion ever. Sadly, Tyson had a very turbulent life in the 80s and 90s, which eventually caught up to him. I remember when Buster Douglas knocked Tyson out in 1990; it was more than an upset. We learned Tyson was not invincible. I also remember when he fought Holyfield and witnessed the ear biting drama on pay-per-view. It was a combination of excitement and horror!

Holyfield Vs. Tyson II Promo

My dad and I couldn't believe what we had just seen. I will say this, I've watched a lot of boxing, and I don't care what anyone says, Iron Mike is the greatest boxer of all time. Tyson in his prime would have crushed anyone before his time, even Ali, and he would crush anyone boxing today. Anyone that says Ali would have beaten Tyson is deferring respect to Ali as a great fighter, but let's be realistic, Tyson (1987-1990) would have dominated— as long as the fight lasted no longer than a few rounds! On November 15, 2024, an unprecedented fight took place between Mike Tyson (58) and Jake Paul (27) at AT&T Stadium in Arlington, Texas. Paul is a former YouTube personality and Disney star who has transitioned into a successful professional boxer. Every Gen Xer was excited about this inconceivable boxing match, and we were all absolutely sure that Mike Tyson was going to knock this kid out. Unfortunately, what we watched was a pure money-grab spectacle that further reinforced everything wrong with boxing a sport today.

Paul Vs. Tyson Netflix Promo

***

Controversial moments? We had plenty! The steroids and cocaine scandal in baseball showed us our heroes weren't perfect. Players like Dave Parker, Keith Hernandez, and Tim Raines testified about cocaine use in Pittsburgh drug trials in 1985. It was a wake-up call about the dark side of pro sports.

I watched the most basketball in my life back in the 80s and 90s. Being from Detroit, I cheered on that rowdy Pistons team, known as the *Bad Boys*. And who could forget the Lakers-Celtics rivalry that defined NBA basketball in the 80s? Do you remember the absolute joy of watching Magic versus Bird? Both basketball legends were stylish and dominant in the sport. The *Showtime Lakers* and the blue-collar Celtics gave us three NBA Finals matchups in the decade (1984, 1985, and 1987). Every playground had its Magic vs Bird vs Jordan vs Ewing vs Thomas!

One of my favorite sports commercials of all time is the 1993 McDonald's *The Showdown* starring Larry Bird and Michael Jordan— "Off the expressway, over the river, off the billboard, through the window, off the wall, nothing but net.

Jordan vs. Bird: One-on-One (Nintendo Entertainment System, 1989)

One of the most important and greatest sports memories of the 80s was the story of Mary Lou Retton and how she became America's sweetheart at the 1984 Olympics in Los Angeles. MLR scored perfect 10s and won gold in the all-around. But more importantly, she showed young girls they could be both powerful and successful. Martina Navratilova dominated tennis with an unrivaled power game, while Chris Evert showed that precision and mental toughness were just as valuable.

The 1984 Olympics in Los Angeles were a coming-out party for American sports dominance, even if the Soviet boycott took some shine off. Carl Lewis matching Jesse Owens' four gold medals was historic. I also think Carl Lewis is the greatest all-around Olympian of all time. While Michael Phelps' record-breaking medal count is undeniable, Carl Lewis' versatility and dominance across multiple events make a strong case for him as the greatest all-around Olympian. Lewis' ability to excel in both sprinting and long jump, winning nine gold medals across four Olympic Games, showcases his extraordinary athleticism and skill.

80s athletics were a wild ride, but the 90s really hit the sweet spot for sports. Production value was increasing and athletes were becoming global brands, but weren't yet curating their personal brands on social media. We were there, now in our teens and twenties, watching it all unfold on cable TV instead of rabbit-ear antennas, drinking beer instead of stealing sips from our parents' Schlitz (my dad was a Johnny Walker Blue Label man).

His Airness, Michael Jordan, dominated the 90s. We watched him three-peat twice (91-93, 96-98), take a baseball sabbatical in between after his father's tragic death, and return with the iconic "I'm back" – the most efficient press release in sports history. The flu game, the last shot against Utah—absolutely blew our mind. I watched that game, and even though I was a Pistons fan, I admired Jordan because he was spectacular to watch. One of my regrets was not being able to watch him live against the Pistons ever, because we just couldn't afford it.

1993 CHICAGO BULLS VS. DETROIT PISTONS TICKET STUB

The 1994 World Series never happened. No, really, it didn't. The baseball strike killed the season and gave us all an early lesson in how labor disputes could ruin sports. But baseball redeemed itself in the most artificial way possible in 1998, when McGwire and Sosa chased Roger Maris's home run record. We celebrated then, even though our BS detectors were pinging like crazy. Turns out those oversized forearms weren't just from eating their Wheaties. Who knew? (We all knew.) Doesn't matter, it was still the best time to watch baseball. I wish the strike never happened though. I believe it took so many of us away from watching baseball for a while, and that was a tragedy. I even stopped collecting baseball cards after that!

We can't talk about 90s sports and not mention Tiger Woods. He showed up at the 1997 Masters and didn't just win — he demolished the field by 12 strokes. The thing about Tiger was that he made golf look cool. Those Nike commercials with "I am Tiger Woods" spoke to something bigger than sports, and we were old enough to get it. I've never been even an enthusiast golfer, but I've enjoyed watching Tiger's career over the years.

1999 Sports Illustrated Magazine TIGER WOODS Major Statement Issue

The NFL gave us the Dallas Cowboys dynasty, with Troy Aikman, Emmitt Smith, and Michael Irvin winning three Super Bowls in four years. We had some incredible football players in the 90s. Joe Montana and the 49ers were still playing well (Cowboys/49ers were the Lakers/Celtics of the NFL), and just look at this roster of greats:

Dan Marino, Joe Montana, John Elway, Troy Aikman, Brett Favre, Barry Sanders, Emmitt Smith, Jerry Rice, Deion Sanders, Steve Young, Thurman Thomas, Michael Irvin, Reggie White, Bruce Smith, Cortez Kennedy, Junior Seau, Derrick Thomas, Warren Sapp, Cris Carter, Marshall Faulk, Warren Moon, Randall Cunningham, Reggie White, and I've got to mention Bo Jackson, who unfortunately had a career-ending injury on January 13, 1991, during a playoff game against the Cincinnati Bengals. My favorite to watch was Barry Sanders though, who left the NFL in his prime, which left us all utterly dumbfounded!

The 1992 Olympic Dream Team was the greatest basketball team ever assembled. The game was a preview of sports globalization. We sent Jordan, Magic, Bird, and company to Barcelona to show the world how basketball should be played. The world took notes, and two decades later, we're not automatically taking gold anymore.

1992-93 Olympic Dream Team USA Basketball Trading Card

Hockey gave us the New York Rangers, finally breaking their 54-year Stanley Cup curse (Dutton's Curse) in 1994. Maybe you weren't a hockey fan, but if you lived anywhere near New York, that celebration was impossible to ignore. In 1994, I was still in High School and my mathematics teacher was a native New Yorker who also was a die-hard New York Rangers fan. We got a healthy serving of Rangers hockey lore from him. I wish I could still remember his name! Meanwhile, Wayne Gretzky was making hockey matter in Los Angeles, which seemed as improbable as good coffee in gas stations.

90s sports weren't without their darker moments. Mike Tyson's fall from grace went beyond boxing and became a morality tale for the 24-hour news cycle. His release from prison, comeback, and ear-biting incident against Evander Holyfield made boxing feel more like a reality show than a sport. We watched it all with a mix of fascination and revulsion, perfect training for today's social media age.

And how can we forget Nancy Kerrigan and Tonya Harding? The attack happened in Detroit, MI– go figure! The knee-whacking heard around the world turned figure skating into a soap opera that even non-sports fans couldn't ignore. It was a preview of how sports and scandal would become inseparable as news media would grow to become more entertainment than real journalism.

The decade ended with Y2K panic and the beginning of the end of the Chicago Bulls dynasty. Jordan's last shot as a Bull to win the '98 Finals was the perfect punctuation mark, not just on his career, but on an era of sports that somehow felt more authentic.

I think we were lucky enough to experience sports back in the day with just enough distance to appreciate the greatness without being distracted by all the hype. Maybe that's why we remember sports from our time so fondly. I think we caught sports at the perfect intersection of innocence and awareness. We were old enough to understand the significance, young enough to still be amazed, and just skeptical enough to see through the hype while still appreciating the genuine magic when it happened.

🎵 "After these messages, we'll be right back." 🎵

ABC Cartoon Bumper

Chapter Thirteen

RIP Saturday Morning Nostalgia

A unified theory of Saturday mornings and the joy today's kids, and future generations, will never experience

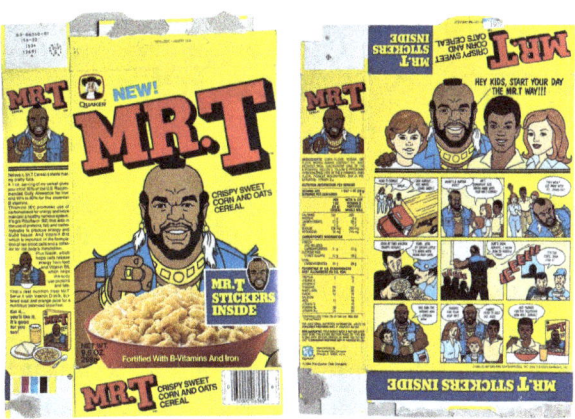

Mr. T Cereal Box

To say that I'm a cereal buff would be an understatement. I have a preferred midnight snack — Mr. T cereal. Since I can't get Mr. T cereal, I mostly settle for Cap'n Crunch.

If you were to ask me what I fantasize about, I'd say it's an absurdly large bowl of Cookie Crisp cereal mixed with a quarter cup of Mr. T cereal swimming in a generous amount of vitamin D milk. I am not at all ashamed to tell you that the best way to truly indulge in a similar taste is to mix Cap'n Crunch and Cocoa Pebbles together and crumble a couple of Keebler cookies into your bowl. Drown them in vitamin D milk. And if you want to get really crazy, toss a few slices of banana in!

Cookie Crisp Cereal Box

Our Saturday Morning Nostalgia Cannot Be Beat!

If there was ever a ritual that connected the life force of a generation, it has to be our Saturday morning routine back in the day, when we woke up early, made a large bowl of our favorite sugary cereal, and watched our favorite Saturday morning cartoons.

Whether it was sitting on the carpet and chomping down on cereal and watching, or placing the bowl on our favorite cartoon tray, or sitting at the kitchen table and reading the back of the cereal box, Saturday mornings were magical.

As soon as the sun peeked through the curtains, we'd leap out of bed, pajama-clad and blurry-eyed. We'd scramble to the living room and turn on the television. We would then rush off to the kitchen. The sweet sound of toy commercials reached our ears, and we went to work preparing the perfect serving of cereal.

Boxes lined up on the kitchen counter or on top of the refrigerator, their mascots grinning at us — Cap'n Crunch, Tony the Tiger, Toucan Sam, Boo-Berry Ghost, Count Chocula, Fred & Barney, Donkey Kong & Mario, and so many more! These weren't just advertising characters, they were also our Saturday morning companions.

Choosing the cereal was a decision of monumental importance. Would it be the chocolate-y crunch of Cocoa Puffs? The fruity circles of Froot Loops? Or perhaps the marshmallow-studded landscape of Lucky Charms? Occasionally, depending on how much cash my dad gave my mom, I'd have to eat a generic puffy rice cereal. Even worse, if my mom had not gone to the grocery store before the next weekend, I might have to eat my dad's Raisin Bran. Yuck!

Bowl filled to the brim, we'd pour in the milk, grab our favorite spoon and we'd make our way to our designated spot in front of the TV. Since Mom's furniture was all covered in plastic, I'd bring my Ghostbusters sleeping bag and crash on the floor.

The ultimate level of synchronization would be to eat cereal from the same cartoon franchise currently on screen. Toys were not the only product advertised through cartoons. I remember eating Bill & Ted's cereal while watching the cartoon!

Bill & Ted's Excellent Cereal Box

We had the greatest lineup of cartoons back in the day. It just kept getting better year after year in the 80s and into the 90s, and then it just sort of died off in the 2010s!

I have four sons of varying ages, so I've seen my fair share of Saturday morning lineups. Currently, my two youngest (6 and 4) watch *Spidey and His Amazing Friends*, but that's pretty much it. Something that has definitely impacted Saturday mornings in my household is little league baseball my sons are involved in. My parents never signed us up for sports when I was a kid, but if watching Saturday morning cartoons was a sport, I'd probably be the Michael Jordan of toon watching!

Here's a list of some of my favorite Saturday morning cartoons from the 1980s and 1990s, including a few obscure shows. Some shows were reruns from past decades, while others aired both weekdays and weekends.

Pee-Wee's Playhouse	DuckTales
The Real Ghostbusters	Hulk Hogan's Rock 'n' Wrestling
Dungeons & Dragons	Mr. T
The Incredible Hulk & Spider Man	Fraggle Rock
Adventures of The Gummi Bears	Teenage Mutant Ninja Turtles
Bill & Ted's Excellent Adventures	Batman: The Animated Series
X-Men	Gargoyles
Pinky and the Brain	Tom & Jerry
Space Ghost	Mr. Wizard's World
G.I. Joe	He-Man and The Masters of The Universe
Thundercats	M.A.S.K.
Heathcliff	Saved By The Bell
Bewitched	ABC Weekend Specials
The Smurfs	Scooby-Doo
Thundarr The Barbarian	Animaniacs
BraveStarr	Garfield and Friends

1989 ABC Saturday Morning Ad Clipping

1980 ABC Saturday Morning Ad Clipping

I still get giddy when I look at this NBC advert! Just thinking about flipping through a comic book and seeing an ad like this is further proof of how incredibly different childhood today is from the time we grew up. Have you looked inside a modern comic book today? If there are ads, they are for modern video games, mainly or a streaming show here and there. There is no childhood joy pouring out of the pages.

Between shows, the commercials were a spectacle in themselves. I never wanted to miss the commercials! We were all about those toy ads, especially the awesome action figures and play sets. We were already making wish lists in our heads!

Remember all the Masters of The Universe toy commercials? Transformers also ruled the commercial space, and so did My Little Pony, Rainbow Brite, and G.I. Joe!

©Mattel/Filmation | He-Man (MOTU) Toy Commercial

©Hasbro/Takara Tomy | Transformers Toy Commercial

©Hasbro | My Little Pony Toy Commercial

You know what else happened Saturday mornings? The grown-ups seemed to fade away and allow us space to enjoy our cartoons. It's like they knew. I think it's because they grew up doing something similar, except for not as cool a line-up of cartoons. And I think my parents wanted to relax Saturday morning, so they let us be. There were no school bells, no homework, no bedtimes looming on the horizon. For those few precious hours, we were the masters of our domain, kings and queens of the living room floor!

I also sat through my fair share of *Rainbow Brite* and *Jem and The Holograms* since I had three sisters at the time that would partake in this Saturday morning ritual.

The spell would break around noon. The cartoons would give way to sports or infomercials, and that was our sign that it was time to go outside and see what our friends were up to.

For generations, Saturday morning cartoons were as much a part of American childhood as baseball and apple pie. However, it's clear that this important ritual has largely faded from the creative minds in broadcast network television. I wrote about the tragic dilution of the past and it starts with people. And I believe the people that ran these networks in the past invested on Saturday morning because they saw an opportunity to promote fun things that kids loved. Today, people working in broadcasting are focused on general content as part of an ecosystem of the streaming network. Everything has become divergent. It's all about streaming.

I will say that changing cultural norms played a significant role in the decline of Saturday morning nostalgia. As families became busier and schedules more fragmented, the idea of a dedicated block of time for children's programming became less practical. As a parent, I'm fairly conscious of screen time, and that's not to say because I believe in some underlying addiction, but there is simply a lot of crap on tv. There just is. I can't blame parents for seeking more educational or interactive activities for their children on weekends.

But I believe one of the more significant factors to the decline of Saturday morning nostalgia is due to increased competition. The rise of cable TV, with dedicated children's channels like Nickelodeon and Cartoon Network, meant that kids could watch their favorite shows any day of the week, at any time. This 24/7 availability of cartoons diminished the special appeal of Saturday mornings.

When streaming services came along, it further sped up this trend. Platforms like Netflix, Hulu, and Disney+ allow children (and nostalgic adults) to access vast libraries of animated content on demand. The need to wait for a specific time to watch cartoons has become obsolete.

Saturday morning nostalgia lay on the foundation of cartoon television. Cereal, snack and beverage, and toy companies flourished because of the full morning of "advertainment" that we took in. Even as an adult, and parent, I still have no problem with advertising of this sort. I understand the ecosystem of entertainment and product placement. Money needs to flow to keep the talent working and the fun programs coming.

Somehow, adults in the past didn't seem to get it. Heavy media regulations were dismantling Saturday morning nostalgia. The Children's Television Act of 1990 and subsequent rules required broadcasters to air a certain amount of educational programming for children. While well-intentioned, these regulations made it more challenging and less profitable for networks to air traditional cartoon blocks. Why wasn't there a compromise? It's so obvious that advertising restrictions and limitations on children's programming made the time slots less lucrative for networks. As profit margins shrunk, networks viewed Saturday mornings as less valuable real estate. Why didn't the network leaders and activists figure out a way to make Saturday morning an eternal rite for all children?

In the late 2000s, children's entertainment was transforming. Everything was shifting towards more live-action and reality programming, which was often cheaper to produce than animated shows. This trend further eroded the dominance of cartoons in the Saturday morning lineup.

1985 CBS Saturday Morning Ad Clipping

1986 NBC Saturday Morning Ad Clipping

1989 NBC Saturday Morning Ad Clipping

There is some good news. I mean, it's ok news.

We can buy most of our favorite cartoons, either on DVD or digitally. I download most of the cartoon content that brings me joy off of YouTube. While the traditional Saturday morning cartoon block may be a thing of the past on broadcast television (I use Hulu live), most of the cartoons we loved live on in new formats. Streaming services and apps have a lot of those animations available. We can create our own Saturday morning experience for our kids. Yes, it's more time consuming, I know, but it's worth it.

I realize for kids from my generation, as well as older Millennials, losing this shared cultural experience is bittersweet. But as long as there's cereal being sold in stores, and I can access the extensive digital library of nostalgic content I've purchased over the years, I'm going to make Saturday mornings a part of my family's tradition. I will be in my pajamas, massive cereal bowl in hand, waiting in anticipation for my next favorite cartoon!

1983 NBC Saturday Morning Ad Clipping

1987 NBC Saturday Morning Ad Clipping

REMEMBER THE CATCHPHRASE?

"I pity the fool!" "WOULDN'T YOU LIKE TO BE A PEPPER TOO?"

"SIT, UBU, SIT... GOOD DOG!"

"AND KNOWING IS HALF THE BATTLE!" "D'OH!"

"HOW YOU DOIN'?" **"NANOO NANOO!"** "AS IF!"

"HAVE MERCY!" "HEY HEY HEY!" "COWABUNGA!"

"UP YOUR NOSE WITH A RUBBER HOSE!" "WHAT YOU TALKIN' 'BOUT, WILLIS?"

"LIVE LONG AND PROSPER" **"DY-NO-MITE!"**

"THE TRUTH IS OUT THERE"

"SURVEY SAYS!" "BOOK 'EM, DANNO!"

"DID I DO THAT?" "HOW RUDE!" "GOOD GRIEF!"

"OH MY NOSE!" "I'VE FALLEN AND I CAN'T GET UP!"

"NO SOUP FOR YOU!"

"KISS MY GRITS!" "THAT'S TOTALLY BOGUS!"

"NOT THE MAMA!" "DON'T HAVE A COW, MAN!"

"HOMEY DON'T PLAY THAT!" "TALK TO THE HAND!"

"SCHWING!" "YO, ADRIAN!" "TIME TO MAKE THE DONUTS"

"I LOVE IT WHEN A PLAN COMES TOGETHER!" "BY THE POWER OF GRAYSKULL!"

"WHO YOU GONNA CALL?" "THIS IS YOUR BRAIN ON DRUGS"

"WHERE IN THE WORLD IS CARMEN SAN DIEGO?" "THEY'RE MAGICALLY DELICIOUS!"

"PARDON ME, WOULD YOU HAVE ANY GREY POUPON?"

"MY NAME IS INIGO MONTOYA-"

NOSTALGIA NATION

Chapter Fourteen
Sights, Sounds, and Feels

I think a lot about the simpler things we did when we were kids. Our generation grew up with some very unique sensory experiences — sights, sounds, and feels younger generations just wouldn't understand. However, I give some of today's kids credit because they are super interested in learning more about the things that made our time unique, even though everything seemed to be noisy, and gloriously inconvenient. Here are a few of those things that will surely take you back!

The Satisfying Click of a Cassette Tape

Remember the distinct "click" when you popped a cassette into your Walkman? What was the first cassette tape you remember buying or listening to?

Bonus points if you ever had to use a pencil to wind a tangled tape back into its case!

The Static-y Glow of a VHS Tape Starting

That blue screen with "Play" in the corner, accompanied by a slight static buzz - it was the universal signal your VCR was about to play your movie! And let's not forget the anxiety of whether someone remembered to rewind the tape!

The Ear-Piercing Screech of Dial-Up Internet

How can we ever forget the robotic symphony of connecting to the internet? That cacophony of beeps and screeches was the soundtrack to entering the digital world - at a blazing 56k speed!

The Battle Cry of "I Have the Power!"

He-Man's transformation was a daily ritual for many kids. The moment Prince Adam held aloft his magic sword, you knew it was go-time against the forces of evil (or time to beg mom for more action figures). I remember rushing home from school most days so I wouldn't miss *Masters of The Universe*!

Filmation | Masters of The Universe (He-Man)

The Clatter of Quarters at the Arcade

The jingle of quarters in your pocket meant serious business at the local arcade. Whether you were lining them up on the *Street Fighter II* cabinet or hoarding them for just one more try at *Pac-Man*, those quarters were your passport to a great arcade experience. Remember running out of quarters and asking your friend for a few? That was a genuine test of friendship!

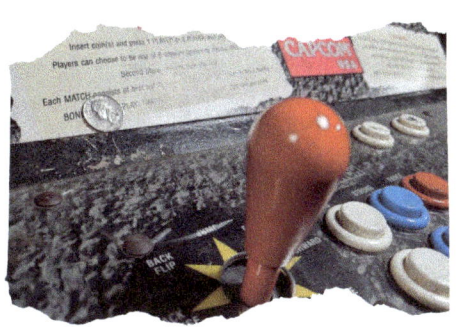

The Crinkle of Opening a Pack of Trading Cards

Whether it was *Garbage Pail Kids* or baseball cards, that crisp sound of tearing open a fresh pack was pure excitement. Would you get that rare card you've been hunting for, or just more doubles to trade? I can't tell you how many packs of 1989 Upper Deck I went through until I got the Ken Griffey Jr. rookie card!

The Clunk of a Cartridge Entering the NES

Blowing on the cartridge, inserting it into your Nintendo Entertainment System, and hearing that satisfying "clunk" - it was the start of a good day. Well, unless the light kept blinking!

What was your favorite game on the NES? Mine has always been *Mike Tyson's Punch Out!*

The Beeps and Boops of a Speak & Spell

This educational toy's robotic voice was both creepy and fascinating. Its monotone "That is correct" was music to any budding speller's ears.

The Whir of a Polaroid Camera

Long before digital cameras and smartphones, the mechanical whir of a Polaroid camera ejecting a photo was magical. Watching the image slowly appear felt like actual sorcery.

The Crackle of Pop Rocks

These fizzy candies created a party in your mouth - and urban legends about what would happen if you mixed them with soda. That distinctive crackling sound and sensation was unlike any other candy experience. You can still buy Pop Rocks today. Try the soda thing!

Beepers and Secret Codes

Hang on, my beeper's blowing up.

Pagers, or Beepers, depending on what you called them, were the ultimate symbol of importance in the 80s and 90s, or at least the illusion of it. Nothing screamed "I'm crucial" louder than a clunky little device buzzing on your hip, begging you to find a payphone like your life depended on it. And let's not forget the secret language of pager codes. There was an entire subculture built around turning upside-down numbers into cryptic messages. "143" meant "I love you," "07734" was "hello," "823" meant "thinking of you," "1432," was "I love you too," "424," was "call me back," "99" or "6000*171647" was "good night," and if you got "911," someone probably needed a ride to Blockbuster ASAP. It was a simpler, more mysterious time when texting wasn't instant, and your cleverness was measured by how well you could decode pager hieroglyphics. The stuff of genius.

The Scratch of Velcro on a Trapper Keeper

I'm not sure there is a more satisfying rip of Velcro than the one on a Trapper Keeper! You know some serious learning, or flipping through your hidden sheets of *Garbage Pail Kids*, was about to happen.

Make sure to visit my social links to watch a video on my Lambo Trapper Keeper from my personal collection!

RAD FACT:

The Lambo Trapper Keeper is still considered the grail Trapper Keeper of the 1980s by many. It was released in 1988.

The Chime of a Casio Digital Watch

That iconic "beep-beep" hourly chime was the bane of every teacher's existence. But for kids, it was a high-tech way to count down to recess or the end of the school day. It was also a way to feel you were like Michael Knight signaling KITT.

Knight Rider Magazine Advert

The Clack of Slap Bracelets

Remember the satisfying "slap" of those colorful fabric-covered metal bands wrapping around your wrist? Slap bracelets were the ultimate 80s accessory, banned in many schools but coveted by every kid. That sharp clacking sound was like a badge of honor on the playground.

The Whir of a Tape Rewinding in a VCR

Before "Be Kind, Rewind" became a nostalgic phrase, it was a necessity. If you had great listening skills, you could tell when the tape was getting close to stopping!

Bonus memory: the moment of panic when you realized you'd forgotten to rewind a rental before returning it to Blockbuster!

The Crunch of Cap Gun Caps and Spring of Dart Guns

Long before concerns about toy guns, ring cap guns and suction toy guns were a staple of 80s and 90s playtime. The sharp "pop" and pungent smell of a freshly fired caps was thrilling. Whether you preferred the roll caps or the individual ones, that satisfying crunch under your thumb was irresistible — so was the perfect thud and stick of the suction suction tips from the spring loaded toy guns!

The Melodic Chime of an Ice Cream Truck

While not unique to the 80s or 90s, the melody of an approaching ice cream truck held a special magic for kids of these decades. That cheerful tune floating down the street on a hot summer day meant it was time to beg mom or dad (genius level was going to both) for some change and chase down a WWF Superstars of Wrestling Ice Cream Bar, or Bomb Pop, or Screwball.

And for the true connoisseurs of sensory sensations from our time: The bleep of a pager going off (for kids with rich parents or aspiring drug dealers), the blip of *Frogger* failing to cross the road, the fizz of opening a fresh Tab Soda, the ding of a typewriter return bell, the hum of a CRT TV warming up, the whir of a rotary phone dial returning, the loud thunk of a TV channel knob changing, the flap and shuffle of card catalog drawers in a library, the hollow *ka-thunk* of a payphone handle being slammed down on its metal cradle, the burning drag of a metal slide on a hot summer day (ouch!), the clink of glass marbles hitting each other, and the winding *zzzip!* of a Fisher-Price View-Master reel clicking into place.

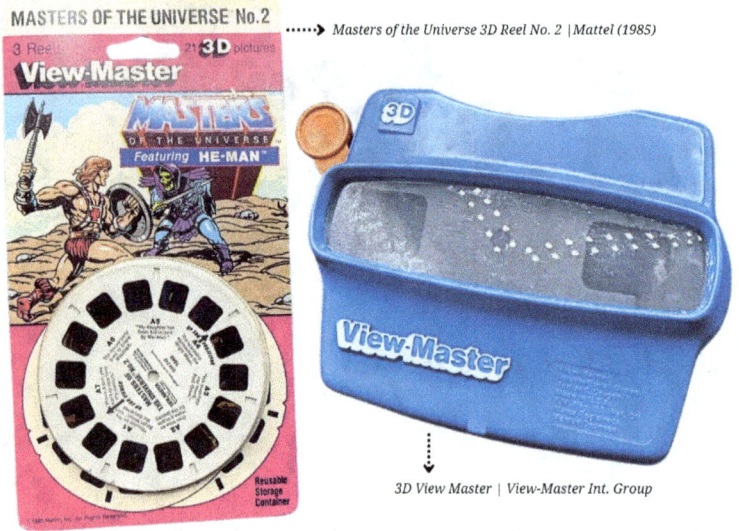

Masters of the Universe 3D Reel No. 2 | Mattel (1985)

3D View Master | View-Master Int. Group

These were the sights, sounds, and feels of a generation raised on minimal supervision and maximum imagination. We didn't just experience life; we *heard* it, *clicked* it, and *clunked* it into existence. When I think back on the past (basically, daily), I look back in fondness on all of these things and more, and I think you probably do too.

"We all lived in the neighborhood for a couple of more years, mostly through Junior High School, and every summer was great. But none of them ever came close to that first one. When one guy would move away, we never replaced him on the team with anyone else. We just kept the game going like he was still there."

Narrator
(The Sandlot - 1993)

Chapter Fifteen

RIP Humanity... & American Neighborhoods

How We Lost Our Sense of Community and Love For Our Neighbors

Remember when you actually knew the people next door?

Some of you still do, and I commend you for that. But for those of you that do, you know, deep down, something's changed — not in a good way.

I'm writing this as a husband and father in my late forties, who now lives in a beautiful San Diego suburb. This is quite the change from my youth, which was spent riding around the blighted neighborhoods of Detroit, MI. Things have certainly changed. Even then, when things were bleakest, I can recall just how much closer we were to our neighbors. We cared for the ones we knew really well, and still looked out for the ones that kept to themselves. I know they did for us.

I steer clear of politics, but I can't help commenting on culture. Having lived through over four decades of highs and lows, I've witnessed countless election cycles. Yet, none has left me as deeply concerned about the state of humanity as in the recent decade. It saddens me to write this, but I believe what follows will resonate deeply with many of you, and that's primarily because, like me, you likely agree that people care less for one another far more today than any other time in recent history.

Let's go back for a bit—

I'm a first-generation immigrant and the oldest of five siblings. When we got to the United States, I had already experienced life overseas (Greece, to be specific). I remember living through the destructive earthquake in Corinth/Athens in 1981, and camping out in the outskirts of the city with all our neighbors as we waited out the tremors. Nearly everything was destroyed, including our small home. I recall the kindness of people experiencing that traumatic event together.

Later that year, we arrived in Detroit, Michigan, where I began assimilating quickly, mainly because my parents were culture shocked. I could tell, even at a young age, that my parents would not transition easily. They were older, and it's extremely more challenging for older immigrants to assimilate quickly. It was my birthday when we landed in the United States. I was exactly five years old, but I knew I would need to grow up quickly.

Every day in Detroit was a struggle. There were times we had one meal only. Somehow, my parents got me registered in school. I think family members and The Red Cross helped, because my parents had no clue what to do. They bought cat food thinking it was tuna, and marshmallows thinking they were cotton swabs. I'm not exaggerating.

I got into scuffles almost every other day. I was behind, still learning the language, and I was a Middle-Eastern kid, "fresh off the boat," as bullies liked to say, so I was low hanging fruit to be picked on. Now and then, a neighbor would come out of their home and they would stop a situation from getting worse if they heard a group of kids yelling at each other. It was like they knew. This happened more than you think off 7-Mile Road and State Fair. By the time I was ten, I'd gotten into so many street fights I'd gotten a reputation for not backing down, so the fighting tapered off slightly. Academics? Forget about it. My sex-ed began around age six or seven, delivered through rain-soaked adult magazines abandoned by addicts along my route to elementary school.

Eventually, when you got big enough, the older kids that loitered around school didn't care about your age. If you looked older, you became a target. During one particularly brutal Michigan winter, the snow fell so heavily that even my father — who believed school attendance trumped all but natural disasters — had to be convinced by my mother to drive me. Back then, it took more than several feet of snow to justify missing a day of education. On our way, we encountered a Lincoln Continental stranded in the middle of the road. Its driver, a burly man in his late thirties, was fighting a losing battle against the snowdrift that had trapped his car. My father, drawing on his military background and electrician's mentality of always being prepared, pulled over without hesitation. "Hop out and help," he said, moving towards the trunk of our old Mercury station wagon, the car he cherished like a member of his family. Armed with a short shovel from my father's carefully maintained emergency kit, we joined the stranger at the front of his Lincoln. While the two men exchanged brief words, my father attacked the packed snow with practiced efficiency. I did my best to help, my gloved hands more enthusiastic than effective, but I suspect my presence was less about the actual shoveling and more about my father's impromptu lesson in preparedness and helping others. Once freed, the grateful driver continued on his way, with us following behind until we reached *Grayling Elementary*. My father dropped me off and headed to work, leaving me with an unspoken lesson that would outlast the winter's deepest snow.

A week later, trudging home from school and trying to avoid the nasty yellow slush that Midwest winter leaves behind, I sensed trouble before I heard it — older kids following me, their taunts loud and clear. The snowballs started flying. Growing up where I did, I was no stranger to fist fights and bullies, but this was different. These were older kids, and they didn't know I was a little kid in a big kid's body. In my neighborhood, some kids would provoke you just to see what you'd do, and I figured that's all this was. I was wrong. They yanked me down, and suddenly my world was nothing but cold slush and pain. Kicks landed everywhere as they jostled me around. I curled into myself, protecting my face, knowing from experience that I just had to wait it out the initial violence. Their laughter cut through the winter air until a thunderous "HEY!" split their laughter.

"Cut that shit out now!" the voice boomed across the yard. Through watery eyes, I saw a large man standing on the other side of the fence, gripping a baseball bat. "He ain't fightin' back, so get your asses outta here right now before I hop over this fence and break this bat off in your ass!"

The bullies scattered, shouting expletives at the man. When I stumbled to my feet to thank my defender, I couldn't believe it — there stood the same burly man with the Lincoln that my father and I had helped the week before. After exchanging thank yous and no problems, he added, "Don't forget to thank your father for helpin' me out last week."

We are all connected to one another.

I never saw those bullies again — a mercy of fate I still appreciate. But that day taught me something far more valuable than the simple relief of avoided violence. At an age when the world was still taking shape in my mind, I witnessed both the darkest and brightest sides of human nature within minutes of each other. While some sought to hurt, others stood ready to protect. This man — this neighbor who owed me nothing — chose action over indifference. In today's world, where people often hide behind phone screens, turning others' pain into social media content, his intervention stands as a testament to a simpler truth: sometimes the universe orchestrates perfect moments of reciprocal kindness, reminding us that every act of goodwill sends ripples we cannot foresee.

Grayling Elementary was set ablaze by vandals on Christmas Eve of 1999, and was heavily damaged. It never recovered after that. It was condemned in 2009 and demolished in 2013.

There were so many more instances like that which showed neighborly care, but it's clearly become a rarity today.

For Generation X and older Millennials, the concept of "community" wasn't just an ideal; it was a lived reality. People knew they shared the same struggles, and families nearby were friendly to one another. It wasn't always perfect. There were instances I knew about where some folks were not friendly, but people said hello, and would sometimes stop to chat with one another about their day and about their kids.

I've observed a decline in people looking up and greeting each other. They just keep on doing their thing, heads down, or glued to their phones. I observe people in lines. They are totally unaware of each other. When I travel, I rarely encounter people who will strike up a conversation. Having traveled since 2004, I've seen a completely different travel culture emerge. Is fear the driving force behind this?

Was it the pandemic? I heard it called the "*Plandemic*." Americans have never distrusted the government more than they do today. There is a major distrust of the media as well.

Liam Walsh | The New Yorker

You would think that as time has gone by, and technology has improved people's lives, that relationships between people would improve. But, it's been the opposite. We are witnessing heightened hostility on a variety of levels, from individuals to nations. I don't write about political things, not because I don't understand them — in fact, I believe I would be a formidable political and cultural essayist (humble brag) — I don't write about these things because humans today have thrown out history and reason. Feelings and personal identity supersede common sense and logic. Much of the distrust stems from corruption and greed of politicians, and powerful corporations that have weaponized race, economics, and the media. Good luck having an opinion out there.

An interesting study on civic engagement and trust, performed by Pew Research Center, found that many Americans link low trust in government and fellow citizens to difficulties in solving national issues, with 70% believing that lack of trust in each other makes problems harder to tackle. There are notable differences in trust levels across demographics, with younger, less educated, and lower-income groups expressing lower trust compared to older, wealthier individuals. Despite the pessimism, 84% of Americans still believe it's possible to improve trust levels through political reforms and community-building efforts.

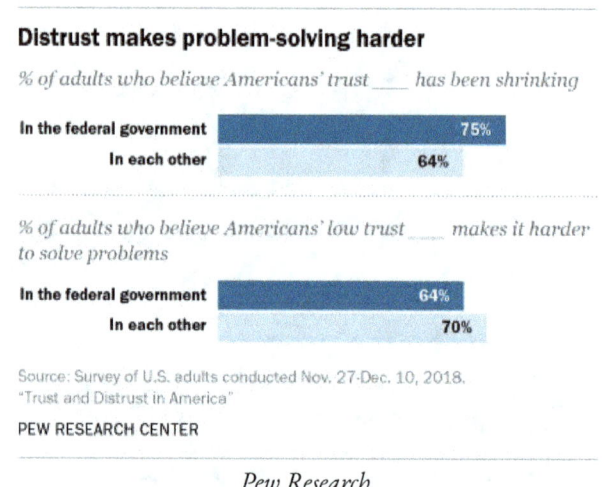

Pew Research

This is part of a <u>longer-term decline in trust</u>. In 1964, 77% of Americans trusted the federal government to do the right thing all or most of the time. There have been a few periods of *increased* trust in the decades since, including shortly after the Sept. 11 terrorist attacks. But since 2008, fewer than 30% of Americans have said they trust the government to do the right thing all or most of the time.

Despite the hardships we faced, when we arrived in the United States in 1981, we knew America was our new home, and we were going to do everything we could to become Americans. That meant something. America symbolized hope, opportunity, and a fresh start. My parents fled economic hardship, political unrest, religious persecution, and they viewed America as a land of boundless possibilities, where hard work and determination could lead to a better life.

There were cultural and language barriers, for sure, but my parents taught us to persevere and to care for those around us. They made a personal sacrifice of leaving their homeland in pursuit of a brighter future for our family. I remember that even when we struggled, our parents reminded us that there were others out there that were going through worse.

Are these sensible and caring ideals being cultivated in our culture today? Can we honestly say that this is the general outlook of society in the America we are living in?

Do those wishing to make a life in our nation still aspire to these principles of caring for their fellow Americans as they work hard toward being more prosperous? Has amassing wealth become the ultimate goal in all our pursuits?

The most hard question to consider is whether our nation's resources are purposefully being mismanaged by the ruling elite for nefarious reasons. What we once knew to be the generosity of the USA has become an expected handout — a strategic tool used by political parties against its own citizens. Several nations have used immigration as a tool to manipulate and destabilize their own societies in the past.

This cultural shift plants distrust, hatred, and anxiety in the hearts of people toward one another. It's difficult to drop all of this frustration on the back of a large government with all the resources to destroy someone's life. Instead, people distrust and mistreat one another. They are less likely to care for their neighbor and more likely to dislike and distrust them.

Is this all on purpose?

What if I told you this is exactly how Rome fell?

Fall of the Roman Empire in painting: Vincenzo Camuccini, La morte di Cesare, 1804-1805, Galleria Nazionale d'Arte Moderna, Rome, Italy.

There's still hope...

Pockets of genuine community still flourish across our nation, often centered around the rhythmic pulse of youth sports fields and gymnasiums where I now watch my own children play. These spaces, like churches, have become modern town squares where families forge bonds over shared sideline emotions and post-game celebrations. It's here, between the whistles and cheers, that neighbors become more than just adjacent addresses — they become part of our extended family's story. When I look back at my childhood, I see now what my younger self simply took for granted: neighbors weren't just people who shared the same zip code—they were vital threads in our social fabric, woven together by necessity and circumstance. We relied on each other not because it was noble or expected, but because that's how communities survived and thrived. Whether it was a baseball bat wielded in defense of a stranger's child or a borrowed cup of sugar during a snowstorm, these connections formed an invisible safety net that caught us when we fell. Today, amid our digital isolation, these face-to-face community bonds become even more precious. In the stands of Little League games or on the sidelines of soccer matches, we're not just spectators—we're participants in an age-old tradition of knitting together the fabric of community, one shared experience at a time. It's here that we rediscover what my childhood knew instinctively: we need each other, not just occasionally, but fundamentally.

My parents were not the social type. They liked to keep to themselves, mostly. But sometimes, my dad would surprise me and he would say hello to a neighbor a block down by name. Our communities had garage sales where you would get to know your neighbor by dropping in to see what they were selling.

In fact, my first Arnold Schwarzenegger book, *Arnold's Bodybuilding For Men*, I picked up from a yard sale our neighbor was having. I learned about our neighbor and got to know their kids that way. I paid a quarter for the book, by the way, and I read it cover to cover too. I recall holding on to it until I was about 30 years old and donated it to the local library.

You didn't just know your neighbor's names; you knew their quirks, their routines, and probably what they were having for dinner.

Remember when borrowing a cup of sugar wasn't just a cliché, but a genuine interaction? It wasn't uncommon to knock on a neighbor's door, not for an emergency, but simply to chat or share the latest neighborhood gossip. As kids, we roamed freely from one backyard to another, and parents kept a collective eye on the tribe of children that seemed to belong to everyone and no one in particular.

The neighborhood was our social network before social networks existed. It was where we learned about life, love, and the importance of community. We celebrated together, mourned together, and navigated the difficulties of life with a support system that extended beyond our immediate family.

But somewhere along the way, things changed. The digital age promised to connect us more than ever, yet paradoxically, it eroded the very fabric of our local communities. Suddenly, it became easier to text a friend across the country than to walk next door and strike up a conversation.

The rise of suburban sprawl didn't help either. As developments expanded, so did our emotional distance from one another. Garages replaced front porches, and fences grew taller. The impromptu neighborhood odysseys on our BMX bikes, and the ritual pilgrimages to whoever's house had the latest gaming console, slowly slipped away. Gone were the days when you'd hear "Mom, I'm going to Billy's to play Nintendo!" echo down the street, replaced by a silence that even the most advanced gaming headsets couldn't fill.

Our lives have all become busier and more hectic. Two-income households have become the norm, leaving less time for neighborhood socializing. The breakdown of the family has contributed to tremendous challenges being felt by all generations around today. This could be a large contributor to the breakdown of kindness. Adversity within families ripples through society.

The irony is that while we've never been more "connected" in a global sense, we've become increasingly disconnected from those physically closest to us. We know more about the lives of Instagram influencers than we do about the family next door. We're more likely to get our sense of community from online forums than from actual face-to-face interactions with our neighbors.

This shift has had profound implications. The erosion of neighborhood connections has contributed to a broader decline in civic engagement and social trust. We're less likely to take part in local government, join community organizations, or even vote in local elections. The delicate ecosystem of neighborhood trust and mutual reliance has eroded quietly, like a shoreline giving way to the tide—not in dramatic crashes, but in the subtle retreat of a thousand small kindnesses once taken for granted.

What does this stem from? Again, I ask, is this on purpose?

The consequences extend beyond just feeling disconnected. Neighborhoods knitted together by genuine connection yield dividends far beyond the obvious. Like a social immune system, strong community bonds not only fight off the virus of crime but nurture the mental wellness of everyone within their reach. Every neighbor who waves, watches, and cares becomes a thread in a safety net that catches us all — sometimes before we even know we're falling.

We have the greatest mental health crisis in recorded history.

So, what can we do to reclaim that sense of community? It starts with small steps. Attempting to introduce yourself to new neighbors, organizing or taking part in community events, or simply spending more time in your front yard instead of your backyard can all help rebuild those connections.

We did these things.

Some communities are taking more organized approaches, creating neighborhood associations or using apps designed to connect neighbors. While these digital solutions might seem at odds with the old-school neighborhood vibe we're missing, they can be a bridge to more meaningful, in-person connections.

The challenge for Gen X and older Millennials is to reconcile our nostalgia for the neighborhoods of our youth with the realities of modern life. We can't turn back the clock, but we can work to create communities that blend the best of both worlds—leveraging technology to facilitate real-world connections rather than replace them.

As we navigate an increasingly complex and often isolating world, perhaps it's time to look to our own backyards (and front yards) for the sense of belonging we crave. The death of the American neighborhood doesn't have to be permanent. With effort and intention, we can breathe new life into our communities, one friendly wave and shared conversation at a time.

After all, sometimes the best way to move forward is to remember where we came from—and the neighborhoods that shaped us.

I challenge you to go say hello to your neighbor. I bet it would shock them. Maybe it will even change their perspective.

We need a neighborhood revival more today than ever.

"One Thing About Living In Santa Carla I Never Could Stomach... All The Damn Vampires."

Bernard Hughes as Grandpa
(The Lost Boys - 1987)

Chapter Sixteen
Trick-or-Treat Gen X Style

A Nostalgic Journey into 80s and 90s Halloween

Each season, as the crisp autumn air settles in and leaves turn, those of us who grew up in the 80s and 90s can't help but feel a twinge of nostalgia for the Halloweens of our youth. It was a time of tremendous excitement, creativity, and sometimes more than just a hint of spookiness that made October 31st the most anticipated day of the year.

Let's set the record straight: Halloween's massive popularity today is thanks to Gen X! As kids, we lived for the candy, costumes, and chaos, and as adults, we've turned it into an epic celebration because we always felt we could have done it better than our parents — especially with all the resources available today. From over-the-top decorations, awesome costumes, and availability of materials available month's before the holiday, we've taken it to the next level.

I'm not sure about you, but my parents hated Halloween back in the day. They called it Satan's holiday. Maybe this was a typical thing in Christian households, because you know, 80s Christian is the most hardcore Christian. But for us kids it was a blast, even if it was simply pairing cheap plastic fangs with toxic face paint that ate through my skin! We just wanted to fit in, and my sisters and I did whatever we could to enjoy the holiday without alarming our parents. Were your parents like this or did they let you enjoy Halloween without making you feel like you were going to go to hell? I get it, there are things that are way over the top today, and definitely some questionable costumes and decorations, but, for the most part, people just like dressing up like their favorite characters and being around friends. And there's always the Harvest Festival at local churches for a safer and more family friendly holiday.

PAAS Makeup Kit (1984)

The Costumes

One of the most thrilling aspects of Halloween was choosing the perfect costume. In the 80s and early 90s, popular choices often reflected the pop culture of the time. We eagerly donned plastic masks and vinyl suits to transform into our favorite characters. He-Man, She-Ra, Teenage Mutant Ninja Turtles, and the Ghostbusters were costumes I remember seeing for years throughout the two decades. For girls, Madonna-inspired looks with lace gloves and teased hair were a hit, while boys often opted for Universal Monster costumes. Central to these memories are the iconic Ben Cooper costumes and masks, which defined Halloween for an entire generation.

Ben Cooper Costume Catalog (1986)

Ben Cooper, Inc., founded in 1937, became synonymous with Halloween for generations of kids, especially from the 1950s through the 1980s. Their simple yet effective costumes—typically a plastic mask paired with a vinyl smock—were the definitive costumes of our childhood.

The appeal of Ben Cooper costumes lay in their affordability and accessibility. We could easily transform into our favorite characters—from superheroes like Spider-Man and Batman to characters like Barbie and Disney princesses. The masks featured vibrant colors and exaggerated features, making them instantly recognizable. While these costumes might seem cheesy or even slightly creepy by today's standards, they were the epitome of Halloween cool for every child. The slight discomfort of wearing a plastic mask that pressed against your face was a small price to pay for the thrill of becoming your favorite character for a night.

Ben Cooper costumes are highly collectible today, with many enthusiasts hunting vintage designs. The company produced an assortment of characters, including classic horror icons and popular figures from television and film. Each costume often came in various box designs, adding to their collectability.

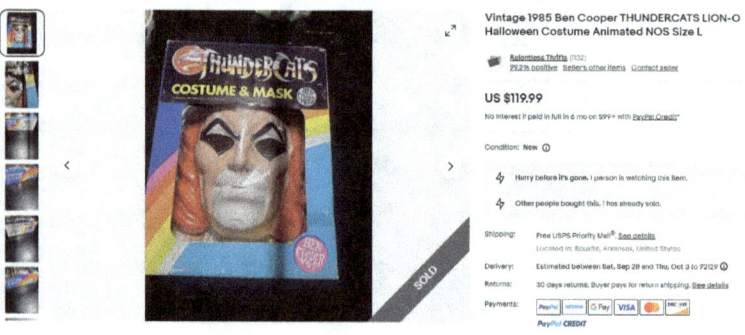

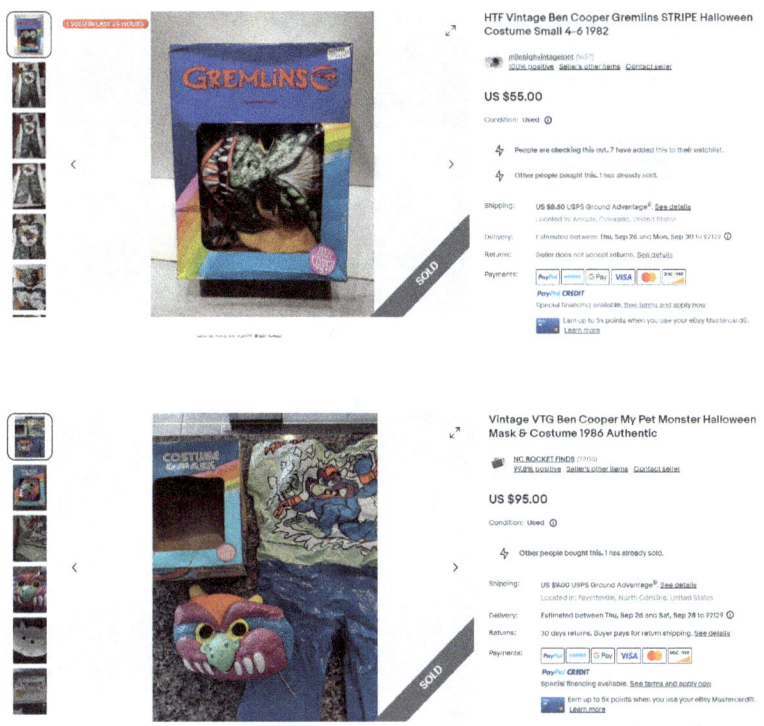

Despite their simplistic design, Ben Cooper masks have a certain nostalgic charm that resonates with those who wore them. They evoke memories of trick-or-treating in noisy plastic costumes while carrying pillowcases, garbage bags, or McDonald's pails for candy collection. For me, I'll never forget the smelly plastic of the mask!

As we rolled into the 90s, our tastes shifted towards more DIY costumes. Armed with face paint, cardboard, and a healthy dose of imagination, we got really creative. Some of us became Nintendo game cartridges, while others concocted amalgamations of various monsters. When Scream hit theaters in 1996, Ghostface masks dominated Halloween. You couldn't walk down a street without seeing that iconic white face. The grunge movement left its mark too, turning Kurt Cobain's signature look into an easy costume choice. Suddenly, everyone's older brother's flannel shirt and torn jeans became the perfect October outfit.

McDonald's Halloween Pails: The OG Trick-or-Treat Flexing

No discussion of 80s and 90s Halloween would be complete without mentioning the McDonald's Halloween pails. First introduced to the public in 1986, these plastic buckets came in three designs: a white ghost named *McBoo*, an orange pumpkin called *McPunk'n*, and a green witch dubbed *McGoblin*. Each year, we eagerly awaited the return of these pails, which served not only as trick-or-treat buckets but also as collectibles.

Oh, and let me add that each kid had to have one of these pails. I absolutely did, so I made sure I was well-behaved and kept the connection to Halloween hidden from my parents. I remember saying they were Happy Meal buckets. We never really fooled them. Oh, the lies we told for the love of Halloween!

Halloween on the Small Screen

Television played a significant role in building Halloween excitement. *It's the Great Pumpkin, Charlie Brown* became an annual tradition for our families, and still is for many Gen X kids. Other Halloween specials like *Garfield's Halloween Adventure* and *The Halloween Tree* also became yearly favorites. I still put these on for my kids every year. I really look forward to these and they seem to always put me in the spirit of the holidays.

As cable TV programs expanded in the 90s, channels like Nickelodeon and Cartoon Network introduced their own Halloween programming blocks. Who could forget *NICK or Treat Halloweenie* or *Cartoon Network's Halloween Eve*?

School Parties Were Our Daytime Halloween Fix

For many of us, Halloween celebrations began at school. The classrooms were decked out for Halloween with orange and black streamers, paper jack-o'-lanterns, and spooky window clings. The class party was always a highlight, with everyone dressed up in costumes and enjoying cupcakes decorated with spooky plastic spider rings and candy corn.

These parties usually featured games like bobbing for apples and pin the nose on the pumpkin. Some schools even organized haunted houses in their gymnasiums, staffed by enthusiastic parent volunteers and a few of the funner teachers!

Home Decorations Were a Must

I'm amazed at how elaborate Halloween decorations are now compared to when we were kids. Halloween decorations in the 80s and 90s were simpler than the elaborate displays we see today. Our homes featured carved pumpkins on the porch, perhaps accompanied by a grinning skeleton or a stuffed scarecrow. Giant inflatable pumpkins and ghosts were among the decorations that became more prevalent in the 1990s.

Inside, we might hang paper skeletons or strings of pumpkin lights. Bowls of candy corn were staples on coffee tables across America.

The blow mold plastic ghosts, witches, and pumpkins stand out in my memory as some of the most memorable decorations. They were cool and sometimes even creepy.

The Great Candy Scare of The 80s

While Halloween was largely a time of joy and excitement, it wasn't without its anxieties. The 80s and 90s saw the peak of parental concerns about tampered Halloween candy. Rumors of razor blades in apples and poisoned candy spread like wildfire, causing our parents to scrutinize our Halloween loot with a fine-toothed comb, which was incredibly annoying.

This fear led to the rise of "trunk-or-treat" events and Halloween parties at community centers, offering a perceived safer alternative to traditional trick-or-treating. However, for us, the thrill of going door-to-door in the neighborhood remained an irreplaceable part of the Halloween experience.

I can vividly remember being told by teachers to watch out for apples with razor blades in them. Maybe this was a Detroit thing? I've even heard stories of poisoned candy. If I brought any candy home from school, my parents were combing through it. These are the same people that would let me play outside until dark, never really checking on me.

Devil's Night

In Detroit during the 1980s, Halloween eve became infamously known as *Devil's Night*, a period marked by widespread arson and destructive behavior that reached alarming levels. This phenomenon was unique to Detroit in its scale and intensity, drawing national and even international attention.

The night of October 30th saw a dramatic spike in intentionally set fires across the city, particularly targeting abandoned buildings and homes. I remember on Halloween Eve my dad would gather us all together for a prayer in our home and he would tell us not to be afraid of anything. I also recall he said he might need to wake me up to help him put out any fires that could affect our home. I remember one Halloween Eve in the early 80s where our front porch lit up in flames and we rushed out to put out the fire. Turns out, someone threw a Molotov cocktail at our house. I was, of course, unaware of its name prior to my father's explanation. One year, our neighbor's place went up in flames.

In 1984, the situation reached its peak, with firefighters responding to a staggering 810 fires over a three-day period around Halloween. This was a massive increase from the typical 50 to 60 fires Detroit would normally experience in a 24-hour period. On Halloween morning, the city was shrouded in an ominous, smoky haze, creating an apocalyptic atmosphere.

While the roots of this destructive tradition lie in earlier, less harmful pranks, its escalation was dramatic in the 1980s. Several factors contributed to this escalation, including rising unemployment, an increasing number of abandoned properties, and a general sense of urban decay. Also, there were a lot of unruly individuals that just wanted to partake in the destructive activities of the night. The situation became so notorious that it attracted "fire buffs" from other states and even countries, who came to witness the blazes firsthand. The city's authorities struggled to contain the problem, leading to the implementation of curfews, increased police and fire department patrols, and eventually, community-led initiatives to combat the destruction.

Trick-or-Treating Was The Main Event

As twilight fell on October 31st, neighborhoods came alive with the sounds of excited children. Armed with plastic pumpkins, pillowcases, garbage bags, or those coveted McDonald's pails, we set out to collect as much candy as possible. The crisp autumn air vibrated with the sound of rustling leaves, children's excited cries of "trick or treat," and the occasional celebratory gunshot from a boisterous neighbor. This was a common occurrence in Detroit. In fact, it was common on every holiday in Detroit.

I couldn't wait to get some of my favorite candies, such as Reese's Peanut Butter Cups, Snickers, Baby Ruth, Milky Way, M&M's, Butterfinger, 100 Grand, Kit Kats, Almond Joy, Mounds, and candy corn. In the 90s, fresh additions like Gushers and Fruit by the Foot added some variety to the typical chocolate-heavy hauls.

Every Halloween night ended the same way — candy bags upturned onto dinner tables or living room floors across America, creating mountains of sugary sweets, and coveted candy bars. Trading took a more serious turn, kids turned into master negotiators. "I'll give you THREE Tootsie Rolls for that bubble gum cigar!" Some swaps got downright intense, like mini Wall Street trading floors fueled by pixie sticks and determination. We'd sort our hauls into strategic piles, guarding our premium candies like dragons protecting gold, while trying to unload those unwanted butterscotch candies and orange-wrapped peanut butter taffy onto unsuspecting siblings.

2warpstoneptune | Halloween (1985)

Halloween Music and Movies

Michael Jackson's *Thriller* was a staple at every Halloween dance, while *The Monster Mash* remained a perennial favorite. Oingo Boingo's *Dead Man's Party* was one that I loved, and Rockwell's *Somebody's Watching Me* was another.

Movie marathons were another crucial part of the Halloween experience. Classics like *Hocus Pocus*, *The Addams Family*, and *Beetlejuice* were in heavy rotation. For those seeking more thrills, slasher flicks like *Halloween* and *A Nightmare on Elm Street* provided plenty of scares.

In the early 90s, one of the best things to ever happen to me was my father getting a cable descrambler, a.k.a., the *black box*. This clever electronic changed my life. I could watch all the pay channels like HBO, Skinemax... ahem, Cinemax, Showtime, and so many more! That meant I could watch horror movies that would never air on standard cable television. It was a game-changer.

Michael Jackson | Thriller (1983)

Halloween Evolved

As we got older, we found other ways to celebrate Halloween. We left trick-or-treating to the kids as we moved on to Halloween parties at home with friends.

My college years at San Diego State marked Halloween's transformation from candy-fueled childhood ritual to full-blown adult spectacle. Our three-bedroom apartment, perched above the Viejas Arena, became party central. My roommates and I earned a reputation for throwing themed ragers that pushed the boundaries of good taste— *Pajama Jammy-Jam* and *A Night in Compton* were just warmups for our legendary Halloween bashes. These weren't your typical college parties; we ran them like a twisted award show, complete with prizes for costumes that hit the sweet spot between creative genius and potential regret. The "most creative," "scariest," and inevitably, "hottest" costume awards became coveted titles that partygoers plotted months in advance to win.

I also remember we attempted to convert the apartment complex into a haunted house. Incredible times for sure.

I'm sure a good part of how I feel about Halloween today compared to the past is nostalgia driven, but I strongly believe Halloween felt raw and real in the past. There were so many unknowns. I feel like today we have everything buttoned up. We know exactly where we are taking our kids, and if we're going to a community or church event, we sort of already know where the candy came from!

Halloween has definitely lost its edge. The holiday has become more sanitized and controlled, and I admit I'm guilty of this too sometimes, that we've prioritized safety over spontaneity. Maybe it's not a bad thing.

Today's Halloween costumes arrive in Amazon boxes, a far cry from the duct-taped, safety-pinned masterpieces we cobbled together from thrift stores and older siblings' closets. The raw creativity born of desperation and limited resources has given way to one-click convenience. Gone are the late-night wanderings and unsupervised adventures, replaced by carefully orchestrated trunk-or-treats and parent-chaperoned events where every shadow has been thoroughly vetted for safety.

My oldest hasn't developed the same appetite for marathon horror sessions that defined my October nights. No staying up late with a bowl of microwave popcorn, watching Jamie Lee Curtis outrun Michael Myers for the tenth time, or debating whether Jason really died in that last *Friday the 13th* sequel. But there's hope — recently, we mapped out our own *Halloween* movie marathon. Starting with John Carpenter's original masterpiece and working our way through the first three Halloween films, maybe throwing in a Friday the 13th for good measure. Sometimes, the best way to bridge generational gaps is through shared screams.

For many of us, this shift feels like a loss of the authentic spirit that once made Halloween a time for adventure and mischief—a night where anything could happen.

But hey, one thing's for sure, and that's not having to worry about Molotov cocktails being thrown on our front porch!

[Ralphie is shoved down the slide, but he stops himself and climbs back up]

Ralphie: No, no! I want an Official Red Ryder Carbine-Action Two-Hundred-Shot Range Model Air Rifle!

Santa Claus: You'll shoot your eye out, kid.

(A Christmas Story - 1983)

Chapter Seventeen
Days of Christmas Past

Things Every Gen Xer Remembers About Christmas Past

Remember when Christmas wasn't a three-month-long assault of targeted ads and algorithmic suggestions? When the holiday season actually waited until after Thanksgiving to kick into gear? For Generation X, Christmas was an extraordinary experience, complete with paper cuts from catalog pages and the constant threat of having to eat some weird concoction of layered gelatin.

The Sacred Texts

The Sears Wish Book was like receiving a new *Jedi* sacred text. We'd spend hours sprawled on the living room floor, creating rings of destruction with our careful catalog studying. Armed with pens, we'd circle every conceivable toy we wanted, knowing full well we'd get maybe two things from our extensively researched lists. The Toys "R" Us catalog was our backup bible, just in case Santa needed options. *"Okay, if I can't have the G.I. Joe Aircraft Carrier, I'll settle for three smaller Joe vehicles and that weird knock-off Transformer."*

The best part? These catalogs were like time capsules of bad fashion and questionable toys. Where else could you find kids wearing matching velour tracksuits while playing with a toy that was clearly going to be recalled by February?

By the way, am I the only one that used pen and not pencil, just in case the deep pencil circles I made somehow faded by Christmas?

Toys "R" Us Holiday Catalog cover (1989)

Montgomery Ward Christmas Catalog (1984)
Masters of The Universe toys interior spread

The Department Store Portrait Ritual

It wasn't an 80s or 90s Christmas if you weren't stuffed into an itchy sweater and dragged to Sears Portrait Studio, where a photographer, who clearly hated their life, would attempt to make you smile by squeaking a rubber duck that had seen better days. The resulting photos always made you look like you were being held hostage by the holiday spirit, complete with that weird blue-gray backdrop that apparently came standard in every department store across America.

Bonus points if your mom made the entire family wear matching outfits. Double bonus points if those outfits involved tartan plaid or reindeer motifs.

JC Penny was another place we went, but I always liked Sears better because they had better electronics and toy options.

Fragile Decorations

Every December, dad would disappear into the attic or basement, returning with boxes of decorations that somehow survived another year of improper storage. The annual tradition of untangling Christmas lights was like a complex puzzle game where half the pieces were burned out and the other half would work fine until you actually hung them up.

Those silk-thread glass ornaments? They were basically beautiful booby traps, waiting to shatter the moment you looked at them wrong. And let's not forget the tinsel – that sparkly environmental hazard that would show up in random places until July.

The rest of the house was a veritable Christmas museum. The holidays weren't complete without those tragic felt placemats — gaudy Santas and geese adorned with loose sequins that shed like seasonal dandruff. Tree skirts made from some mysterious synthetic fabric that probably violated several environmental protocols, scratching against your legs every time you reached for a present. Those ceramic trees with their plastic bulbs glowing in radioactive colors still haunt estate sales today. And let's not forget the ultimate symbol of holiday obligation — those giant metal tins of stale popcorn and cement-hard cookies, clearly designed for people you had to give something to but didn't actually like — the perfect passive-aggressive gift that said "I remembered you exist, barely."

Of course, no Gen X Christmas was complete without the nativity scene, usually comprising figurines that had been moved, lost, and replaced over the years. Inevitably, baby Jesus would go missing early on, leading to a full-scale investigation and a hastily placed spare figurine that never quite fit right.

The TV Specials

Before streaming and on-demand viewing, we had one shot to catch our favorite Christmas specials. Miss *Rudolph the Red-Nosed Reindeer* or *A Charlie Brown Christmas* and you'd have to wait an entire year to see it again. The *Fall Preview* issue of TV Guide became a strategic planning document, with multiple backup plans, in case someone forgot to set the VCR timer correctly. Ours was always blinking!

And let's talk about those Rankin/Bass specials – they were basically fever dreams set to music. *The Year Without a Santa Claus* gave us the Heat Miser and Snow Miser, two characters who definitely inspired some future therapy sessions.

I'm still a huge fan of the Rankin/Bass Claymation specials. Both *The Island of Misfit Toys* (Rudolph) and *Nestor, the Long-Eared Christmas Donkey*, are among my favorites.

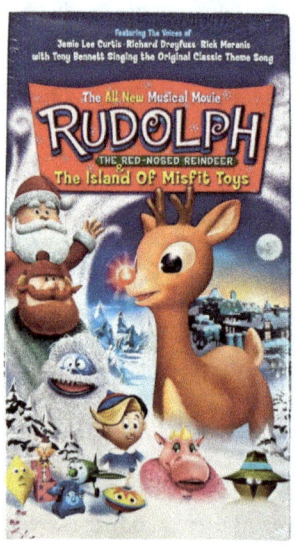

Hanna-Barbera's Holiday Takeover

Every cartoon character in the Hanna-Barbera universe apparently had a Christmas special. *The Flintstones, The Jetsons, Yogi Bear* – they all got in on the action. These specials usually involved some convoluted plot about saving Christmas, because apparently the holiday was perpetually in danger during the 80s and 90s. Who knew that years later that scrooge-like politicians would pose the greatest threat to the holiday?

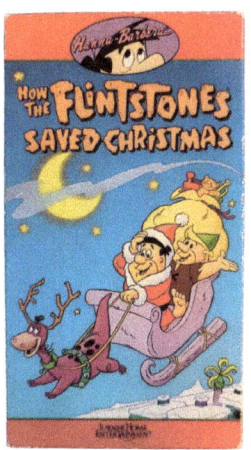 

Mickey's Christmas Carol

Disney's take on the Dickens classic was many kids' first exposure to both Mickey Mouse and existential dread. Watching Scrooge McDuck learn about mortality while being haunted by his dead business partner was quintessential Christmas. It was basically *This Is Your Life* meets *Scared Straight* for waterfowl. *Mickey's Christmas Carol* is still a must-watch for me every season, similar to *It's A Wonderful Life* and *A Christmas Story*.

Christmas Plates Were Serious Business

And no Gen X Christmas was complete without a pilgrimage to grandma's house, where every spare surface was covered in collectible Christmas plates. There were the classic Currier & Ives designs, depicting quaint winter scenes with horse-drawn sleighs. The Precious Moments plates featuring big-eyed children frolicking in the snow, the boy carrying a Christmas tree over his solider. And who could forget the coveted Hallmark plates, each one a masterpiece of seasonal schmaltz, complete with embossed holly leaves and a glittery border. Grandma would display these prized possessions with pride, dusting each one reverently and back them with lace doilies for maximum festive effect. Of course, we were forbidden from touching them, lest we invoke the wrath of "Nana" and her carefully curated Christmas collection.

The Commercial Breaks

The Christmas commercials that aired during those days were an event unto themselves. A few of my favorite Christmas commercials include the Hershey's Kisses Christmas bells, 7UP "Cool Spot" Christmas commercial, Pepsi vs Coke truck drivers, Folgers 'Peter' comes home for Christmas, Campbell's Soup snowman/kid, Ronald McDonald ice skating, and the Fruity/Cocoa Pebbles Fred and Barney and Santa commercial. And let's not forget those endless perfume ads that made absolutely no sense but somehow made you want to smell like a forest in winter.

The Great Mall Santa Pilgrimage

Getting your photo taken with mall Santa was a rite of passage that usually ended in tears – yours, Santa's, or both. The line was always endless, the fake snow was probably asbestos, and Santa's beard looked like moths had attacked it. Yet somehow, these photos became treasured family heirlooms, proudly displayed alongside the Sears portraits.

Ugly Sweaters Were... Normal?

Christmas sweaters weren't an ironic novelty back then – they were a serious fashion statement that usually involved appliqued snowmen or reindeer with actual jingle bells attached. These sweaters were invariably made from some synthetic material that could survive a nuclear winter and would make you sweat in sub-zero temperatures.

The Annual Clothing Pilgrimage

For many of us, Christmas was the one time of year when we got new clothes. This meant spending the week after Christmas trying to break in stiff new jeans and figuring out how to work your new wardrobe into the school social hierarchy. Most of us showed up to school in January wearing everything we got at once!

Every year, right before Christmas, my parents loaded my sisters and me into the Mercury station wagon and headed off to neighboring Ohio to do Christmas at Woolworth's. This was one of my favorite things to do during the holidays. I knew we were going to get some new clothes... finally! Also, Woolworth went hard during Christmas and it was a really special place.

Weird Food? Yes, please!

Jell-O Advert 1980s

Christmas dinner was a time machine of questionable culinary choices. Jell-O molds containing suspicious fruit combinations. Green bean casserole topped with those weird fried onions that only existed during the holidays. Aunt Suzie's "special" fruit cake that we always feared was left over from last year.

And let's not forget the cookies – sugar cookies cut into shapes that became unrecognizable during baking, decorated with enough red and green sugar to put a reindeer into a diabetic coma.

Gift Wrapping Was A Science!

Back in the pre-gift-bag dark ages, wrapping presents was a contact sport that demanded geometric precision, supernatural patience, and at least three paper cuts per gift. Every family had that one wrapping wizard, usually an aunt or grandmother, whose presents looked like they'd been professionally wrapped by origami-trained elves. Each corner was crisp enough to draw blood, every seam invisibly sealed, and bows that defied the laws of physics. Meanwhile, your own wrapped gifts looked like a gang of caffeinated raccoons had handled them, complete with mysterious bulges, tape patches visible from space, and corners that somehow sprouted extra sides. Back then, character gift wrap was childhood currency wrapped around cardboard tubes. The holy grail for me was that *Masters of the Universe* wrapping paper. I never convinced my parents to buy it, which might've been a blessing in disguise. Knowing my collector's tendency, that roll would've ended up preserved in my closet like some ancient scroll, deemed too precious to actually use on mere presents.

Flammable Christmas Stockings

Remember those glorious clear plastic and mesh atrocities that passed for Christmas stockings? Nothing said "festive fire trap" quite like hanging what was essentially a melted shower curtain molded into a stocking shape two feet from actual flames. They had all the charm of a dentist's waiting room and the structural integrity of a grocery store bag, yet somehow our parents thought these transparent hazards (some were mesh sewn onto plastic handles) were the height of holiday sophistication. We all just seemed to ignore how one errant spark could light up the entire mantle!

More Holiday Hazards

Something that sticks out vividly in my memory, and I'm sure yours as well, are the magnificent monuments to petrochemical progress that were the front lawn army of hollow blow-molded Santas and deranged-looking snowmen, their dead-eyed stares illuminated by a single sad light bulb from within. These bad boys were indestructible enough to survive nuclear winter, yet somehow still caved in on one side after a light breeze. The best were those life-sized choir carolers, their faces permanently frozen in some strange expression, slowly fading to a jaundiced yellow over decades in someone's garage. And I will never forget those giant candles with the eternal flame, perpetually tilting like the Tower of Pisa, their fake plastic "drips" collecting actual spider webs until they looked like some Tim Burton fever dream. The pièce de résistance was always that one neighbor who'd arranged them in such density that their yard looked like a clearance sale at a western hardware store.

The Great Annual Battery Search

Each year brought some new electronic promise of the future. The Walkman gave way to the Discman. Nintendo became Super Nintendo. Every device required over a dozen batteries, it seemed, which were never included and always impossible to find in the house on Christmas morning.

Duracell Battery Advert (1983)

The Aftermath

December 26th was like the holiday equivalent of a hangover. Half the toys were already broken, the tree was shedding needles faster than a nervous Welsh corgi, and you had to write thank-you notes to relatives for gifts you'd already lost or broken. For me, and I'm sure countless others that prayed for an NES system, we just wanted to go play *Mike Tyson's Punch Out*, and leave the mess behind!

But somehow, despite the commercialism, the awkward photos, the itchy sweaters, and the questionable food choices, the Christmases of our past were something special. Maybe it was because we had to wait for things, and nothing was certain. I mean, I could circle a hundred different toys in multiple catalogs and what I got for Christmas was a rubber Voltron knockoff (this actually happened). The thing is, I cherished that toy.

Or maybe it's just that everything looks better through the frost-covered lens of nostalgia. Either way, those Gen X Christmases taught us valuable lessons: patience, the art of tactful disappointment, and how to pretend you love a gift while plotting its trade with your neighbor!

The thing is, even to this day, a part of me still wants to circle every toy in a catalog, just for old times' sake.

Buttercup: We'll never succeed. We may as well die here.

Westley: No, no. We have already succeeded. I mean, what are the three terrors of the Fire Swamp? One, the flame spurt - no problem. There's a popping sound preceding each; we can avoid that. Two, the lightning sand, which you were clever enough to discover what that looks like, so in the future we can avoid that too.

Buttercup: Westley, what about the R.O.U.S.'s?

Westley: Rodents Of Unusual Size? I don't think they exist.

[Immediately, an R.O.U.S. attacks him]

(The Princess Bride - 1987)

Chapter Eighteen

The Totally Real (and Totally Not) Fears of Our Youth

We faced some "serious" threats as kids. Forget nuclear war (though, that was an actual real scary thing), our biggest worries involved creatures from the deep, shadowy government conspiracies, and substances that could swallow you whole. And Soviets... we can't forget about Soviet invading forces!

I think it's important we revisit these existential crises that kept us up at night and haunted our dreams... and day dreams.

Quicksand

Quicksand. Just the word conjures images of slow, agonizing suffocation, a fate sealed by slowly sinking into a viscous, inescapable trap. Thanks to countless cartoons, adventure movies, and maybe even a dramatic scene from *The Princess Bride* — and even a more dramatic (and traumatic) one from *The Neverending Story* (although that was a swamp), we believed that quicksand was a legitimate threat, lurking in every seemingly innocent sandy patch. We pictured ourselves, à la Indiana Jones, struggling hopelessly against its relentless pull, our cries for help muffled by the sucking sands. The reality? While unpleasant and potentially dangerous, true quicksand is relatively rare, and escaping it is far easier than Hollywood would have you believe (though, probably best to avoid it).

The Princess Bride (1987)
20th Century Fox

The Bermuda Triangle: Where Planes and Boats Go to Die

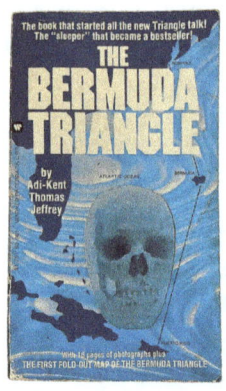

Be honest, how many Bermuda Triangle books did you read back in the day? I feel that anything about The Bermuda Triangle at the Scholastic Book Fair had a magnetic pull on me! This infamous patch of ocean, roughly bordered by Bermuda, Puerto Rico, and Florida, was the stuff of nightmares. Thanks to countless documentaries (and the sheer mystery surrounding disappearances), we believed that some supernatural force – aliens, time warps, or even a grumpy sea monster – devoured unsuspecting vessels and their hapless passengers. Books like *Bermuda Triangle* by Adi-Kent Thomas Jeffrey, and the documentary by Charles Berlitz fueled our anxieties.

While unexplained disappearances occur in the Bermuda Triangle, they are not any more frequent than in other heavily trafficked ocean areas. The mystery, however, keeps the legend alive.

Aliens: They're Among Us (Probably Not, Though We Weren't Sure)

Let's be honest, the 80s and 90s were definitely the golden age of alien invasion stories — although I would argue we've had some really close ones recently. *Close Encounters of the Third Kind* drummed up some paranoia, and I would say *The X-Files* was a high point in alien suspense. Our generation was practically conditioned to believe that extraterrestrial life was not only real but actively interested in, if not outright hostile towards, humanity. We scanned the skies for UFOs, convinced that the government was hiding the truth – a belief perfectly encapsulated by *Independence Day*.

Please tell me you remember the awesome television show, "*V*" — remember when Diana eats the rat?!

While the existence of extraterrestrial life remains a subject of scientific debate, the mass alien invasion predicted by so many films never materialized. (At least, not that we know of...)

Loch Ness Monster: Nessie's Reign of Terror

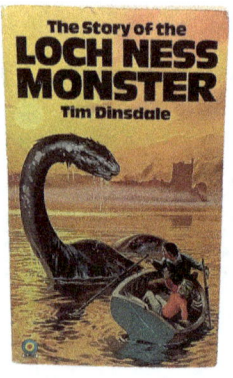

Nessie. The elusive Scottish monster, a gentle giant in some portrayals, a terrifying leviathan in others. Thanks to blurry photographs and countless documentaries (yes, we watched them all); we grew up believing that a plesiosaur-like creature lurked in the depths of Loch Ness, occasionally surfacing to terrify unsuspecting tourists. The mystery surrounding Nessie's existence fueled years of speculation and fueled our imaginations. While many believe in her existence, scientific evidence remains inconclusive. And while our friends overseas had Nessie, we were rightfully afraid of getting into the water thanks to *Jaws*!

Bonus fear unlocked:

Do you remember the films *Piranha II: The Spawning* (1982) and *Alligator* (1980)? These films instilled a deeper fear in me of being in the water. We had the lakes in Michigan where I grew up, but honestly, I knew little about saltwater vs freshwater creatures as a kid, and so I assumed anything could pull me under or leap out of the water at me, if I wasn't careful, including genetically modified piranhas!

Bigfoot: The Elusive Sasquatch

Bigfoot, Sasquatch, the Abominable Snowman — call him what you will. This hairy hominid captivated us. From grainy photos to eyewitness accounts (many of them, let's be honest, possibly fabricated for fun or publicity), the legend of Bigfoot has persisted. Shows like *In Search Of Bigfoot* with Leonard Nimoy heightened the mystique, suggesting that Bigfoot was more than just a tall tale. The evidence, however, remains circumstantial. While the belief persists, the scientific community remains skeptical.

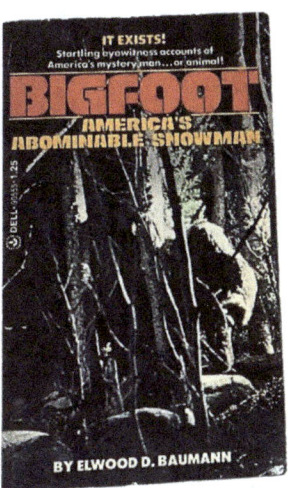

Let's Talk Soviets

The pervasive fear of Soviet invasion during the Cold War fueled anxieties far beyond mere political posturing. Movies like *Red Dawn (1984)*, with its depiction of a brutal, guerilla war fought on American soil against a technologically advanced enemy, tapped into a deep-seated societal unease. This wasn't simply about ideological conflict; it was a genuine fear of a muckier, less-glamorous war than the sanitized narratives of previous conflicts suggested. The imagined invasion wasn't a clean, swift takeover, but a protracted struggle for survival against a seemingly unstoppable force, blurring the lines between civilian and combatant, and leaving behind a landscape of destruction and uncertainty.

Fortunately, things got better, at least for a couple of decades.

Looking back, it's humorous to see the dangers we perceived as children. These fears, catalyzed by the media we consumed, shaped our childhoods, and fueled our imaginations. To tell you the truth, I think I've got a great alien invasion story in mind that I've stored up for over three decades — maybe I'll be able to share it one day!

Quicksand, the Bermuda Triangle, aliens, Nessie, and Bigfoot may not be the menacing threats we once imagined, but they certainly added a thrilling dose of fear to our youth — memories we can now look back on with a smile.

🎵 **We didn't start the fire
It was always burning, since the world's been turning
We didn't start the fire
No, we didn't light it, but we tried to fight it** 🎵

Billy Joel
(We Didn't Start The Fire - 1989)

Chapter Nineteen
The Years That Made Us

The Significant Events and Headlines That Shaped Gen X

I'm so grateful that our generation caught the last wave of shared media experiences before everything fractured into a million digital pieces. When something big happened, we all watched it on one of three networks, read it in actual newspapers or magazines, or heard it within friendship or family circles. I'm also very grateful that I had a television in my room. My parents sort of just let me be. You could say I was a conduit for passing along information. I soaked up everything I saw and heard, making me a natural choice to write for the school paper. I wrote for the school paper for a brief period.

Here are a few of the most significant events of our generation — the ones that likely shaped our worldview, and every Gen X kid remembers.

***

The decade kicked off with the **Iran hostage crisis** and the launch of *Nightline*. Every night, Ted Koppel would come on to remind us how many days Americans had been held hostage (444 in total). We didn't fully grasp the geopolitical implications, but we understood the counting. It was our first taste of how news could become a running serial, complete with its own theme music and graphics. When the hostages were finally released during Reagan's inauguration in 1981, it felt like a season finale. We all exhaled.

National Museum of American Diplomacy (January 20, 1981) | The Hostages Return

Speaking of Reagan, someone tried to assassinate him in 1981. Many of us were sitting in school when the TVs were rolled in. As Reagan exited the Washington Hilton Hotel after a speech, John Hinckley Jr. opened fire, striking the president, his press secretary James Brady, a police officer, and a Secret Service agent. Reagan's quick thinking and the swift actions of his security detail likely saved his life. While recovering from his injuries, Reagan famously quipped to his doctors, "Honey, I forgot to duck." Hinckley was found not guilty by reason of insanity and committed to a mental institution. In June 2022, a judge lifted all court-mandated restrictions on Hinckley, allowing him to live without supervision. He is currently using platforms like YouTube to share his music and artwork publicly.

***

Less than two months after the attempted assassination on Reagan, someone tried to assassinate The Pope. On May 13, 1981, Pope John Paul II's regular Wednesday audience in St. Peter's Square turned into a moment that shocked the Catholic world when Turkish assassin Mehmet Ali Ağca fired four shots at the pontiff from close range. As the Pope was greeting crowds from his open-top Fiat "Popemobile," two bullets struck him in the abdomen, while others injured two bystanders. The Pope collapsed into the arms of his secretary, and the normally bustling square erupted into chaos as Vatican security apprehended the gunman.

The 60-year-old pontiff, who had been pope for less than three years, lost nearly three-quarters of his blood and underwent five hours of emergency surgery at Rome's Gemelli Hospital. His survival was considered miraculous, and he later credited the Virgin Mary of Fatima for saving his life, noting that the attempt occurred on her feast day. In a remarkable act of Christian forgiveness that captured the world's attention, the Pope later visited Ağca in prison in 1983 and publicly forgave him. The assassination attempt only increased John Paul II's global influence and popularity, though he would carry the physical effects of the shooting for the rest of his life. Conspiracy theories about the attack's connection to the Soviet bloc and the Cold War persisted for years, with some suggesting Bulgarian intelligence services had orchestrated the attempt.

***

1984 could have been a quiet year, but On January 27, what should have been a routine commercial shoot for Pepsi turned into a horrific accident that would forever impact Michael Jackson's life and career. During the sixth take of filming at the Shrine Auditorium in Los Angeles, a pyrotechnics display misfired as Jackson was descending a staircase performing *Billie Jean*. The sparks ignited the singer's heavily sprayed hair, and for several seconds, the King of Pop continued to dance, unaware that his head was engulfed in flames. The incident was caught on camera, showing the terrifying moment when Jackson's head became a torch of fire before crew members rushed to extinguish the flames.

Michael Jackson was big news in the 80s, and I remember just how much press this story got!

The accident left Jackson with second and **third-degree burns on his scalp**, requiring extensive surgeries and triggering what many believe was the beginning of his dependency on painkillers. The accident resulted in a $1.5 million settlement from Pepsi, which Jackson donated to the Brotman Medical Center in Culver City, where he was treated. They established the Michael Jackson Burn Center in his honor. The incident marked a pivotal moment in Jackson's life; many close to him noted he was never quite the same afterward, both physically and emotionally. The severe burns and subsequent medical treatments were reportedly factors in his changing appearance and his complex relationship with pain medication in the years that followed.

The Paducah Sun article (1984)

***

On January 28, 1985, the biggest names in American popular music gathered at A&M Recording Studios in Hollywood for a remarkable all-night recording session that would become one of the most significant charitable events in music history. ***We Are the World***, written by Michael Jackson and Lionel Richie, brought together 45 superstars including Bruce Springsteen, Cyndi Lauper, Bob Dylan, Diana Ross, and Ray Charles to raise money for African famine relief. The session began late at night after the American Music Awards, with producer Quincy Jones hanging a sign at the door that read "Check your egos at the door," setting the tone for this unprecedented collaboration.

The resulting single sold over 20 million copies worldwide and raised more than $63 million for humanitarian aid. The chorus of "We are the world, we are the children" became an anthem for global unity and compassion. *We Are the World* took the concept of celebrity fundraising to new heights. The project marked one of the first times American pop culture united so powerfully for a humanitarian cause.

LIFE Magazine | We Are the World (APR 1985)

***

The Space Shuttle Challenger disaster in 1986 was the first time I'd actually seen my classmates cry at school. It was really sad, and I remember our teacher crying as well. We watched it live in our classrooms because Christa McAuliffe was going to be the first teacher in space. The image of that Y-shaped cloud formation is seared into our collective memory. For many of us, it was the moment we realized that progress came with terrible risks, and that sometimes there were no good answers to "why did this happen?"

NEWSWEEK Magazine | Space Shuttle Challenger (1986)

***

In October 1987, 18-month-old Jessica McClure (known to the world as "Baby Jessica") fell 22 feet down an abandoned well in her aunt's backyard in Midland, Texas. The tiny eight-inch diameter pipe trapped the toddler for 58 hours while the entire nation watched the rescue attempt unfold through unprecedented round-the-clock media coverage on CNN.

The rescue effort was extraordinarily complex because of the narrow width of the well and the need to drill through solid rock. Hundreds of rescuers worked continuously, drilling a parallel shaft and then a horizontal tunnel to reach Jessica. I know our family and the entire country were riveted by the ordeal, and Baby Jessica's fate, listening to her singing Winnie the Pooh songs to keep herself calm in the well. After two and a half days, rescuers finally brought her to safety on October 16, 1987. Though she suffered gangrene that led to the loss of a toe and has some scars from her ordeal, Jessica survived and has lived a normal life. Jessica got married in 2006. Her family grew with the arrival of a son in 2007, followed by a daughter in 2009. Today, Jessica dedicates her time to assisting a special education teacher at an elementary school in Midland, Texas. The incident marked one of the first major news events that demonstrated the power of 24-hour cable news to unite the nation around a single story.

PEOPLE Magazine | Baby Jessica (1987)

***

The fall of the Berlin Wall in 1989 was surreal. We'd grown up with the Wall as this immovable symbol of the Cold War, practicing duck-and-cover drills in school (because apparently, a desk would protect us from nuclear annihilation). Then suddenly people were taking sledgehammers to it while David Hasselhoff sang about freedom. It was both profound and absurd, but when that happened, we knew the world was really changing.

> "Mr. Gorbachev, tear down this wall!"
>
> ~ Ronald Reagan

The Wall Came Tumbling Down | Berlin Wall and the Fall of Communism by Jerry Bornstein (1990)

***

The 90s opened with CNN's revolutionary coverage of the **Gulf War**. In 1990, Iraq, under Saddam Hussein's rule, invaded and occupied Kuwait. This aggressive act sparked a swift and decisive response from a coalition of 35 nations, led by the United States. The resulting conflict, known as the Gulf War, aimed to expel Iraqi forces from Kuwait and restore its sovereignty. Remember those green-tinted night vision shots of anti-aircraft fire over Baghdad? It was the first war broadcast live, 24/7. The entire thing was bizarre. We watched smart bombs go down chimneys with surgical precision, making war seem almost clean and video game-like. We should have known better, but the technology was mesmerizing.

It's striking how history often repeats itself. As I write this, Russia's invasion of Ukraine (Feb 2022) echoes the events of the Gulf War (Aug 1990), yet the international response has been notably different. While the world rallied against Iraq's aggression, the global reaction to Russia's actions has been more divided and less decisive. Or was the main issue the oil? It's intriguing to consider the role of oil in shaping international responses to aggression. With the Gulf War, Iraq's invasion of Kuwait threatened the global oil supply, a crucial resource for many nations. This economic threat likely galvanized the international community to take decisive action.

However, Russia's invasion of Ukraine, while also impacting global energy markets, has not triggered a similar level of unified condemnation.

Topps Desert Storm Trading Card (1991)

***

Then came the LA riots in 1992, sparked by the Rodney King verdict. The footage of his beating by LAPD officers was probably the first viral video, though we didn't have that term yet. When the riots erupted, we watched Los Angeles burn on TV, saw Reginald Denny pulled from his truck, and realized that the racial divisions we thought were improving were actually festering.

There have been many politicians, corporations, actors, and athletes that like to say, "end racism," but much of this is virtue signaling. It's easy to say it and go back to making millions of dollars or return to their comfortable lifestyles. The fact is, racism will always fester and will always exist. People can barely tolerate each other in sports stadiums. Professional sports fandom, which should be a source of community and excitement, seems to take a dark turn far too often today. Tragically, almost every season across major sports leagues, we witness incidents where a fan's misguided passion leads to violence, resulting in serious injuries or even fatalities. This troubling phenomenon stems from an artificially cultivated "us versus them" mentality, where loyalty to "our city" and "our team" is elevated to an almost tribal level. Meanwhile, attempts to address societal issues like racism through superficial gestures, such as slogans on jerseys, helmets, or billboards, seem woefully inadequate. While well-intentioned, these efforts fail to address the root causes of discrimination and may even trivialize complex social problems. It's baffling to observe how some individuals place undue faith in such simplistic approaches to resolve deeply ingrained societal issues.

Time Magazine | "Can We All Get Along?" Rodney King Issue (1992)

***

One of the craziest things I remember from the 90s was the David Koresh drama. The Branch Davidian siege in Waco was like watching a slow-motion train wreck over 51 days. We'd tune in each night to see if anything had changed, only to watch it end in flames on April 19, 1993. It fueled conspiracy theories and anti-government sentiment that would have devastating consequences in Oklahoma City two years later.

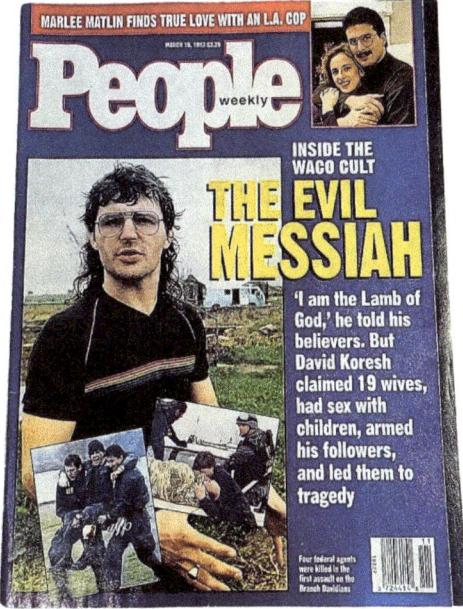

People Magazine | The Evil Messiah (1993)

***

Speaking of Oklahoma City, the 1995 bombing of the Alfred P. Murrah Federal Building shattered our sense of domestic security. The image of that half-collapsed building, and learning that Americans could do this to other Americans, was a gut punch. When we saw firefighter Chris Fields carrying out the lifeless body of one-year-old Baylee Almon, it became our generation's equivalent of the Vietnam War's *Napalm Girl* photo.

Pulitzer Prize-winning photo taken by Charles Porter IV on April 19, 1995 in Oklahoma City, Oklahoma following the bombing of the Alfred P. Murrah Federal Building. The photo was distributed by The Associated Press.

***

But nothing dominated the news quite like the O.J. Simpson saga. The Bronco chase on June 17, 1994, was peak shared experience—97 million people watched it live. NBA Finals? Interrupted. Pizza delivery orders? Skyrocketed. We all knew exactly where we were when that white Ford Bronco cruised down the 405. The subsequent trial was like a soap opera written by John Grisham, starring characters too outrageous for fiction: Kato Kaelin, Judge Ito, Marcia Clark, Johnny Cochran ("If it doesn't fit, you must acquit"). It was the first reality show masquerading as news, complete with daily cliffhangers and plot twists.

Los Angeles Times | Simpson Not Guilty (1995)

***

Then there was the Clinton-Lewinsky scandal, which felt like O.J. 2.0, but with sex instead of murder. We learned more about cigars than we ever wanted to know, and the phrase "I did not have sexual relations with that woman" became both a punchline and a lesson in careful parsing of language. The subsequent impeachment proceedings were like a civics lesson mixed with a tabloid story.

Newsday Long Island (1998)

***

But nothing prepared us for Princess Diana's death in 1997. In the early hours of August 31, 1997, Princess Diana died in a tragic car crash in Paris's Pont de l'Alma tunnel that shook the world and forever changed the British monarchy. Diana, her companion Dodi Fayed, and driver Henri Paul were killed when their Mercedes, being pursued by paparazzi photographers on motorcycles, crashed at high speed inside the tunnel. The "People's Princess," as she was known, was just 36 years old. Even those of us who claimed not to care about the royals felt this one. Maybe because we'd watched her fairy-tale wedding as kids, followed her evolution into the "People's Princess," and understood her struggles with media attention and public expectations. 2.5 billion people watched her funeral worldwide. Elton John reworked *Candle in the Wind*, and we all pretended we weren't crying when he performed it.

USA Today Newspaper | Farewell Diana (1997)

***

The 90s closed with a tragedy. The Columbine shooting in 1999 changed everything about how we viewed school safety. We'd had school shootings before, but this was different — planned, filmed, engineered for maximum media impact. The image of students fleeing with their hands up became tragically iconic, and the phrase "trench coat mafia" entered our lexicon. We didn't know it then, but this would become a horrific template for future tragedies.

TIME Magazine (DEC 1999)

***

What made these events particularly impactful for Gen X was our unique vantage point. We were young enough to be deeply affected, but old enough to understand the implications. We watched the news transform from a dignified evening broadcast into a 24/7 entertainment machine. CNN, launched in 1980, went from being the *Chicken Noodle Network* to the go-to source for breaking news. Every major story brought a new innovation in coverage:

- The Gulf War gave us live war reporting

- O.J. gave us gavel-to-gavel trial coverage

- Monica Lewinsky gave us scandal saturation

- Columbine gave us wall-to-wall tragedy coverage

We witnessed the birth of the modern news cycle, where stories didn't just break—they consumed all media oxygen until the next big thing came along. We saw how coverage shaped narrative, how narrative shaped public opinion, and how public opinion could shape events.

News technology evolved with us. We went from reading about news in the morning paper to watching it unfold live on TV to discussing it in early internet chat rooms. By the end of the 90s, we were getting news online, though we still had to wait for that dial-up connection to complete its screeching handshake with destiny.

But hey, at least we knew what we were watching was real. No one had invented deep-fakes yet!

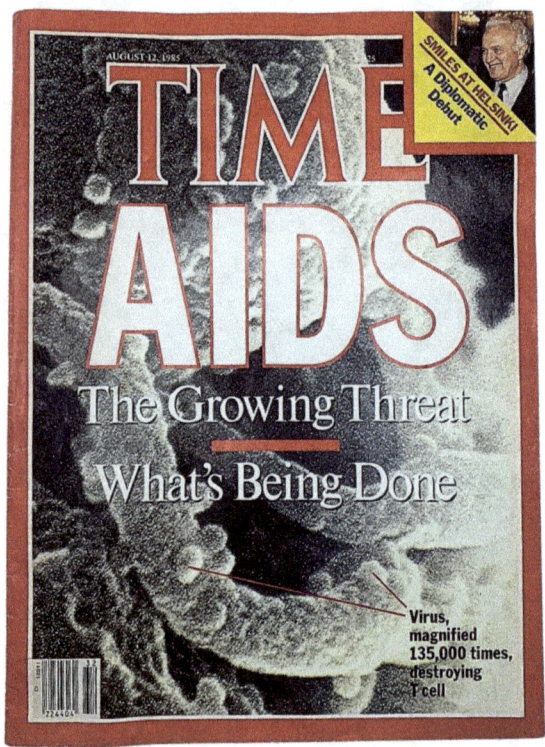

TIME magazine | AIDS Issue (1985)

"Life moves pretty fast. If you don't stop and look around once in a while, you could miss it."

Matthew Broderick as Ferris Bueller
(Ferris Bueller's Day Off - 1986)

Chapter Twenty
The Future of Nostalgia

So what's next for nostalgia?

The last four years have been marked by rapid change and global uncertainty, and as a result, nostalgia has become a comforting anchor and escape for many. From 2020 to 2024, we've witnessed a surge in retro revivals and a fury of nostalgic nods across pop culture and entertainment. Content creators often ask me where nostalgia goes from here. Will it last?

If you've been on social media at all the last few years, you've witnessed the rise of accounts that curate nostalgia. You may be surprised to learn that many of these accounts are run by young adults from all around the world. I know of several accounts run by teens still living with their parents!

I'm sure you've also heard of YouTube Faceless channels. Overseas studios looking to cash in on nostalgia run many of the most successful ones. They have teams using AI and producing video content rapidly. People are eating it up daily because they want to retreat to the past mentally. Who can blame them?

But what are we gaining from this? Does it matter that these faceless accounts are not genuine and just cashing in on an audience that loves the past?

The future of nostalgia as content is certainly a touchy subject, but what I enjoy about the present day is there are significant nostalgia-driven events and trends that are real, and they are introducing the past to the youth today. Which is critical.

***

The 2K Renaissance

Newsweek Magazine | GEN Z (2019)

Something that has recently fascinated me is the success of 2000s nostalgia. The 2000s serves up some serious nostalgia, and they have made a triumphant return on social media. Zoomers are feeling nostalgic far sooner than we did. Could it be that they are facing a bleaker reality than we had foreseen during our time? Could it be that because information flows so much faster today that they are feeling hopeless, and they are reminiscing on the simplicity of the recent past? Remember, everything seemed to change in the 2010s when smartphones were getting smarter, and WiFi was becoming more accessible. Instagram wasn't the most dominant social media platform, and silly, short dancing videos were not yet cannibalizing feeds. Kids that grew up in the 2000s to 2010 experienced the remnants of simpler times. They were still watching many of the cartoons and television shows that rolled over from the late 90s. Gen Z can continue to be proud of their nostalgia and some really wonderful shared experiences.

Given the crisis of independence their generation faces and their growing awareness that technological progress may not guarantee a bright future, I believe the younger generation will be a powerful force in fostering nostalgia, but for less positive reasons. This is undeniably a sad reality.

***

Stranger Things To Rule Them All

MAD Magazine #548 December 2017 | Stranger Things Issue

Netflix's *Stranger Things* is returning for its final season in 2025. The show will continue to be a juggernaut of 80s nostalgia throughout the year. From its synth-driven soundtrack to its nods to 1980s pop culture, the show has resonated deeply with viewers of all generations. The show's influence has gone beyond the screen, impacting fashion, music, and even product design. There are even annual tributes now all over the world during Halloween dedicated to custom-built *Stranger Things* tribute sets. A house in San Diego, close to where I live, has become famous for creating elaborate sets every Halloween as a tribute to Gen X films and shows.

Stranger Things' success has sparked a wider trend of 80s-inspired content across various media platforms, including cinema. *The Barbie Movie* is one example. I believe *Stranger Things* will be the most nostalgic media property twenty years from now. What do you think?

The show skillfully engages with pop-culture from our time by incorporating a wealth of Easter eggs in each episode, creating a nostalgic viewing experience that resonates with fans. It effectively markets itself to younger audiences through dynamic outreach on social media platforms, enhancing its appeal and fostering a vibrant online community.

Harry Potter has been a very successful franchise overall. But I believe the Stranger Things universe will be much more successful over the course of the next three decades. Both universes are expansive, but *Stranger Things* appeals to a broader spectrum of generations, and frankly, the monsters and protagonists are far superior. Don't come at me, Potter heads!

***

Reboots and Revivals

The Ultimate Guide to Jurassic World (August, 2022)

We've witnessed a ton of remakes, many terrible ones, over the last twenty years, but since I dove into social media in 2020 into the present, there have been an unprecedented number of reboots, revivals, and spin-offs of incredibly memorable franchises. Shows like *Friends: The Reunion*, the *Sex and the City* revival, *That '90s Show* (a spin-off of That '70s Show), *Fuller House, Quantum Leap, Party of Five, The Wonder Years*, and animation reboot of He-Man, titled, *Masters of The Universe: Revelations* (created and produced by Kevin Smith), all tapped into viewers' nostalgia.

In cinema, famous franchises have seen new installments that bridge the gap between original fans and new audiences. Films like *Ghostbusters Afterlife/Frozen Empire, Jurassic World Trilogy, Top Gun Maverick, Indiana Jones and The Dial of Destiny, Scream, Roadhouse* (Jake Gyllenhaal), *Beverly Hills Cop: Axel F, Coming 2 America, Halloween, Bill & Ted Face The Music, Hocus Pocus 2*, and *Beetlejuice Beetlejuice*. These revivals often blend nostalgia with contemporary themes. Some are better than others, but they certainly offer a comforting familiarity.

I believe we will continue to see reboots drop as streaming grows, and there are over a dozen film remakes and world expansions on the horizon. For example, *Highlander, Short Circuit*, and *Police Academy* are all in development as I write this book!

Being a movie buff, I'm all for it. I love the original films, and like many of you, I'm not a fan of remakes. BUT– I'm totally for universe expansion and extended stories built upon the franchises we grew up watching. For example, I absolutely disliked the newer *Indiana Jones* flicks, but I've really enjoyed the new *Alien* films. *Alien: Romulus* (2024) blew me away! It's not just another sequel, it's a standalone story that expands the universe, and I loved it.

***

Physical Media Forever!

In an unexpected twist, physical music formats have experienced a significant resurgence the last few years. Vinyl records, in particular, saw a dramatic increase in sales, with both new releases and reissues of classic albums driving the trend. Have you tried to get your hands on a copy of New Order's album *Substance*? Prior to 2020, you could easily get one for around $10, but by 2022 copies of the album were selling for over $50!

Cassette tapes have also made a surprising comeback, especially among indie artists and collectors. Once again, as the younger generation continues to engage with the past, it's natural for them to explore the media we grew up using. I see new accounts pop-up on social media, run by young people, that are strictly devoted to cassette culture. While I admire it, I'm also conscious of the fact they are the reason demand has gone up for physical media, and the increase in cost of acquiring vintage media.

The same goes for compact discs. Influencers showing off their audio set up are a dime a dozen. There are plenty that are CD-centric, especially on YouTube. Compact Discs are still being made, so this format of physical media will probably still be around for years to come.

I think the greatest challenge to physical media of the past is the hardware component. If VCRs and cassette players were still being manufactured in large quantities, we might see a dramatic shift in purchasing media. This may still happen.

DVDs are also very popular today. I still buy them regularly. DVDs are probably the most common form of physical media being purchased regularly, and because of that, there have been many independent boutique production companies that have entered the scene, producing highly stylized versions of older films, chalk-full of bonus features. Several that come to mind include Vinegar Syndrome, Shout/Scream Factory, and Arrow Video. One of the most well known is Criterion. Something I got into heavily in the 90s was watching old samurai flicks. In the 1950s and 1960s, Akira Kurosawa made some of the most spectacular samurai flicks ever! The films were popular in Japan, but it took roughly twenty to thirty years before they really gained notoriety in the United States. The primary reason — they were released on vhs format and made available for rental stores all over the country. By the 90s, every cinephile knew about Kurosawa's samurai flicks. To this day, one of the most sought after DVD releases from Criterion is its 1998 release of *The Seven Samurai*. Early on, Criterion was at the forefront of including and producing special feature content on its DVD releases. For me, this was the time frame when I started really collecting physical media with extended material on DVD, CD, and VHS.

Even today, as I expand my collection, I seek physical media that has special features. I usually stay away from generic releases because I can easily find the content on digital.

The allure of physical media lies in its tangible nature and the unparalleled value it offers. Beyond the content itself, collectors enjoy exclusive special features and the peace of mind that comes with unrestricted access, free from the whims of streaming platforms. Unlike ephemeral digital files prone to loss or corruption, physical media — be it vinyl records, DVDs, or books — provides a tactile connection and enduring accessibility. For Generation X, elder Millennials, and a new wave of collectors alike, the ritual of handling, storing, and enjoying these items fosters a profound sense of ownership and nostalgia. This physical interaction creates a more immersive and personal experience, allowing enthusiasts to curate their own cultural archives and relive cherished moments at will.

You know the craziest thing is the licensing agreements between studios and streaming services. Films and shows come and go from a streaming service based on internal agreements between companies, and as consumers, we're never sure if we have access to a piece of content unless we own it.

I remember my dad complaining about the cable bill back in the day. Today, our parents would be shocked at the amount we pay for several streaming services, so we have access to their programming!

Ok, so how do I prioritize what I buy digitally, don't buy and enjoy through streaming, versus what I buy in physical format?

It's pretty simple, actually. Any film, music, or book that I absolutely loved as a kid, I try to buy in physical format — if the price is right. If the price is not right, I will try to source it in digital format to own. If I'm not in love with something, and maybe it doesn't bring me a ton of joy, I just enjoy it on streaming.

With vinyl, I am extremely particular. The piece has to be in great condition, must have all the artwork and content, must be from the 80s or 90s, and should be affordable. I don't buy into hype or over priced items. I make offers for something I really want.

For DVDs, I try to stay with Bluray for now, or previous special editions. I think 4K is great if you have the hardware, but I don't mind the graininess of non-4K releases. We were watching those far before 4K was around. I try to pre-order often to save money, and I have to be interested in the film or a particular franchise to purchase it.

I hope this helps you make informed buying decisions if you're interested in getting into physical media.

Tears For Fears "Songs From The Big Chair" LP/Vinyl (1985) MERCURY

***

Nostalgic Gaming and Streaming Experiences

Super Mario Bros. Movie Poster

The gaming industry has always leaned heavily into nostalgia. Remakes and remasters of classic games have become increasingly popular over the last few years, with both *Final Fantasy VII* and *Tony Hawk's Pro Skater 1+2* remakes receiving critical acclaim and commercial success.

I believe Nintendo will continue to capitalize on its rich history. Did you see *The Super Mario Bros. Movie* (2023)? Nintendo has really flourished over the last few decades. I firmly believe its next console will be revolutionary and will usher in a new generation of retro gaming lovers.

Something I've really enjoyed seeing is the release of miniature versions of classic consoles and bringing classic franchises to new platforms. The popularity of retro-style indie games has also surged, with pixel art and chiptune music really taking us back!

And we can't forget the impact of mobile gaming on nostalgia! Classic franchises like Sonic the Hedgehog, Final Fantasy, and Pokémon have seamlessly transitioned to mobile gaming. As a retro gamer myself, I absolutely love how mobile gaming is bringing a new generation of gamers into the retro worlds we loved. These mobile adaptations offer bite-sized experiences, nostalgic callbacks, and innovative gameplay mechanics. Sonic's lightning-fast dashes and iconic loops have been reimagined for touchscreens, while Final Fantasy has delivered both nostalgic remasters and original mobile adventures. *Pokémon GO* took the world by storm, blending augmented reality with the iconic monster-catching franchise, encouraging players to explore the real world and catch virtual creatures (sometimes in a very annoying way, I have to admit).

***

The Streaming Wars and Content Libraries

As streaming platforms proliferated over the last few years, the battle for subscribers has often centered on nostalgic content. Services like Disney+ leveraged its vast library of classic cartoons, movies, and TV shows, while others invested heavily in acquiring the rights to popular sitcoms and dramas from previous decades.

It seems like there's a new streaming network hitting the scene every year, sometimes even more. I see a few things happening over the next ten years, one of them being a consolidation of networks in order to compete with the likes of YouTube. YouTube is currently being watched by more people than any other streaming network out there. Why is that? Well, it's because we each bring our own unique experience and personality to our channel. And because of this, I believe networks will have no choice but to merge, as well as create opportunities for independent creator channels (similar to YouTube), and they will also cater to segmented audience interests, especially nostalgia.

Do you remember the TV Guide Channel? One of the most frustrating things we dealt with back in the day was missing the description of what was playing on the channel we liked best, and then having to wait for what seemed like forever to have another shot at reading the description when the channel got back around again — which was basically forever!

***

Retro-Inspired Brand Campaigns

Have you noticed the increase in nostalgia-driven commercials airing during major sporting events? Marketing strategies across various industries will continue to tap into the power of nostalgia. Major brands will continue to revive classic logos, packaging designs, and advertising campaigns to evoke positive emotions and build stronger connections with consumers.

In the last few years alone, companies like Coca-Cola, Gucci, Adidas, Nintendo, Old Spice, and Converse have tapped into their past to sell products.

I also believe we will continue to see more and more well-recognized tv and film actors from the past appear in televised commercials, just as we've seen over the last several years. I would love to see the *Star Trek: The Next Generation* cast show up in a SpaceX commercial!

Influencers Being Influencers

With their power to create trends and alter behavior, influencers are primed to affect the way we feel about nostalgia in the years to come. On the one hand, they can curate and amplify nostalgic content, sparking widespread interest in the past. Influencers will continue to share vintage fashion, music, and pop culture references. I see an explosion of comedy related nostalgia as well. After all, there are a lot of hilarious things we experienced in the past that we can laugh about. All of this will lead to new trends, from fashion to home decor, and even inspire a new generation to appreciate classic art, literature, and film.

However, there's a potential downside to this influencer-driven nostalgia. My biggest concern is with short-sighted creators that stir up controversy for followers and likes. There are nefarious forces out there creating more than just political divide between people in our society. I'm noticing a worrisome trend of "Intergenerational Trolling" (a Gen Divide) taking place in online forums, especially within social media apps. One generation is bashing another because of economics, politics, values, or all those things. It's really concerning, and you should be concerned about it too. Remember, we are quickly becoming the oldest living generation, and that places us in the crosshairs of emotional activists, and even worse, disgruntled influencers taking out their frustrations on older generations.

I've seen Gen X influencers do it too!

The fact is, we are all in this together. There will always be political, economic, and societal challenges, but we must care for one another, and in the words of James Dalton (Patrick Swayze in *Roadhouse* – 1989) — "BE NICE."

THE END....

Kind of.

thank you

I truly hope you enjoyed Nostalgia Nation! If this book brought back great memories or gave you a new appreciation for the past, I'd be incredibly grateful if you took a moment to leave a review on *Amazon* and/or *Goodreads*. Your words help others discover and enjoy this book too — thank you for being part of this journey!

WHAT'S NEXT?

As I reached the last pages of this book, I found myself overwhelmed by the wealth of memories and moments that remained untold. How could I possibly capture every defining event and detail of the two decades that changed the world and shaped our lives?

This book represents just the beginning of our journey through the 80s and 90s. I feel very satisfied that I've established a definitive chronicle of growing up Gen X as a framework, and I expect future editions or expansions will be necessary in order to explore more esoteric topics like the birth of indie film culture, a more nuanced look of morning line-ups, such as Reading Rainbow, 90s "trash tv," the transformation of television from three networks to hundreds of cable channels, and countless other moments that defined this remarkable period.

I invite you to join me on this ongoing exploration of our shared past. Follow me on social media or visit my website www.that80sdude.com for regular updates, bonus content, and previews of upcoming chapters. I create short retrospectives and other videos on my YouTube Channel (80s Dude TV) as well as post interviews with actors, musicians, and other talented people that shaped the pop-culture of our generation.

Share your own memories and stories in the comments section of my weekly newsletter - they might just find their way into the next volume. After all, these aren't just my stories; they belong to all of us who lived through these transformative years.

The journey continues...

ACKNOWLEDGMENTS

Writing a book is never a solitary journey, even when you spend countless hours alone with your thoughts and your keyboard. This book emerged from decades of memories shaped by friends and family. Conceptualizing this book was extremely challenging. Where do I even start? Which topics do I include? When I searched for other books like the one I wanted to write, I couldn't find any. So, I thought someone needed to create a chronicle for our generation. There was plenty of information online, but I knew it would be important to start with my story and have the rest grow out of that. I can tell you it was not easy to write this book, and I spent a lot of time organizing it and sweating over what should absolutely be included and what could wait for future iterations. This pressure of getting everything in a book was heavy, but it helped to weave my personal experience into it.

That said, there was no way I would have attempted writing this book without being sure that I had the support of my family. Most importantly, my wife, Bethany. She's not only my anchor but also my best friend, incredible mom and stepmom, and the most patient person in our marriage.

I owe a special thanks to my mom and dad, and my four sisters. They not only shared these decades with me but also helped me recall many of the little details that made these times so unforgettable. Their stories, photographs, and support helped to bring this narrative to life. I am eternally grateful to my parents for their incredible sacrifices. Their courageous decision to leave their homeland and build a new life in America has given me opportunities beyond measure. I owe everything to them.

I've been incredibly lucky to have Ammar J. (Mark) as my best friend since we were young kids in Detroit. We bonded over our shared love for pop culture and became like brothers (a great thing for me, coming from a family of four sisters). He always pushed me to be better and believed in me. I'm so grateful for the shared experiences we had biking to Taco Bell, the baseball card shops, and the comic book stores we hung out at. We spent so much time playing Dungeons & Dragons. He's been an amazing friend and inspiration throughout my life. He will always be my brother from another mother!

My deepest gratitude goes to the historians, archivists, journalists, content creators, and photographers who documented these moments as they happened. Despite having lived through this amazing period, writing a book like this still required a lot of research, especially for specific dates. Your contemporary accounts and images helped jog my memory and helped me accurately capture the spirit of each moment.

I extend my sincere thanks to Lisa Downs, who wrote the foreword to this book. Lisa is a gifted director and producer known for her captivating and insightful documentaries exploring important films from our childhood. Her upcoming project, *Life After The Goonies*, is eagerly anticipated. Lisa, thank you for your friendship and your invaluable contributions as a true ambassador of nostalgia.

I want to take a moment to express my deep love and gratitude for my children, who have inspired me to preserve these memories. Your laughter at my stories and your curiosity about how I navigated the 80s have motivated me to write this book and share these experiences with the world. Your interest in what life was truly like during my youth has been a driving force behind this project.

This book is for my fellow Gen Xers — the totally awesome people who bridge the past and the present. I'm truly proud to be a Gen X kid, and I feel really blessed to have been born in this era.

Thank you to my friends in the nostalgia communities online for supporting my projects, and for your dedication to our shared memories. I also want to say a special thank you to those of you that are representing Gen X at home and sharing these memories with your kids. Let's keep the memories alive — Nostalgia matters!

ABOUT THE AUTHOR

John Toma was born in Baghdad, Iraq and is a first-generation immigrant. He and his parents fled the Middle-East in 1979 in search of a better life. John grew up in Detroit, Michigan in the 80s — the oldest of five children — growing up way too quickly and living on television, where he developed an encyclopedic knowledge of 80s pop culture that would eventually prove completely useless — until now. These days, John writes the popular weekly newsletter *Nostalgia Nation*, having somehow convinced over half a million social media followers that remembering stuff is cool. John currently lives in San Diego with his family. When he's not reminiscing about the good old days, you can find him enjoying his vintage collection, indulging in retro gaming, and teaching his four sons that baseball is far superior to social media.

www.ingramcontent.com/pod-product-compliance
Lightning Source LLC
Chambersburg PA
CBHW050524100526
44581CB00006B/117/J